the well-worn interior

robin forster and tim whittaker

the well-worn interior

stewart, tabori & chang

NEW YORK

Copyright © 2003 Robin Forster and Tim Whittaker

First published in the United Kingdom by Thames & Hudson Ltd., London.

Published by
Stewart, Tabori & Chang
A Company of La Martinière Groupe
115 West 18th Street
New York, NY 10011

Canadian Distribution:
Canadian Manda Group
One Atlantic Avenue, Suite 105
Toronto, Ontario M6K 3E7
Canada

Library of Congress Cataloging-in-Publication Data
Forster, Robin.
    The well-worn interior / Robin Forster and Tim Whittaker.
      p.   cm.
    Includes bibliographical references.
      ISBN 1-58479-307-4
              1.   Antiques in interior decoration. 2. Interior
decoration—History. I. Whittaker, Tim. II. Title.
      NK 2115.5.A5.F67 2003
      747—dc21   2003045860

The text of this book was composed in Myriad
Design by Thames & Hudson

Printed in Singapore

10 9 8 7 6 5 4 3 2 1
First U.S. Printing

'Many people may reproach me for judging my fellow-man in this way, by a trifling and external criterion, and they will remind you that clothes do not make the man, and therefore the house does not describe the man who lives in it. But I would prefer to apply another famous saying: *Le style est l'homme même*. The house is the man: *tel le logis, tel le maître*, or if you prefer "tell me how your house looks and I'll tell you who you are".'

Mario Praz, *An Illustrated History of Interior Decoration*, 1964

contents

introduction

the timeless appeal of the well-worn interior

Peeling paint, tatty wallpaper, faded fabrics and battered floors have an intrinsic beauty and softness that reflect their history, testaments to years of habitation, vestiges of the ravages of light and time. If we ignore the dictates of conventional taste, we can uncover the charm and appeal of the faded and gently decaying interior.

This is a book for those interested in patina, a character so often lacking in modern homes and so frequently destroyed by restoration, which through overearnest re-creation can often sanitize the very atmosphere it is trying to preserve. In being renovated, an old building can lose its integrity, becoming a present-day ideal of what it is thought to have been, a misplaced twenty-first-century perspective of the past. If we can resist the urge to paint over the past, to straighten and tidy up, then we enjoy and appreciate a building's evocative historic atmosphere and individual – if not idiosyncratic – beauty that truly are the spirit of the place.

Underlying the ideas presented in this book are principles of conservation: repair and patch when necessary, do not needlessly remove original material and save as much old fabric as possible. By studying and understanding the materials of the past – how they were applied or used, how they have withstood the test of time – we can genuinely capture our often neglected old houses and dwellings.

Searching out unrestored gems across the globe , this book features delightfully patrician eighteenth- and nineteenth-century townhouses in London, Dublin, New York and Charleston (South Carolina) and magical country residences in England, Ireland, France, Germany, Italy and the United States. We focus on the untouched, the romantic and the unusual, illustrating regional styles and practices and exploring the materials and techniques, such as limewash, flat oil paint and graining. How these elements are put together often defines the look associated with a particular country, but the style and decorative ideas contained in most of these interiors are at home anywhere in the world. A number of the houses are open to the public through historic preservation societies (see p. 190 for addresses), while others are private, rare interior realms that have been lovingly maintained over decades, if not generations.

We also consider the history of building elements. The repair and maintenance of an old house require care, sensitivity and attention to detail, and in today's do-it-yourself world, the well-intentioned home owner is often at the mercy of conflicting advice and a building-materials industry with a bewilderingly vast range of products. To understand your house and its history, local reference libraries or regional and national archives are a good starting point, but much can be gleaned from the building itself.

A true grasp of your house's evolution will aid you enormously to make suitable alterations or modernizations that complement the existing building, whether adding a conservatory, applying a fresh lick of paint, or re-organizing the interior spaces. You will also be able to identify the correct materials and style to employ when patching and repairing what already exists. The building itself contains clues that allow the owner to interpret its

age and history, including any alterations or later additions to the original building. Often with just a little detective work, you can place your home in a local and historical perspective that will help you determine the features that are either typical or rare for their period.

The older your house the more likely it is to be built from locally obtained materials, such as stone or timber. The degree of a material's pliability and the local climate usually establish regional variations. For instance, in some areas of the United States and Europe, old chimneys on houses and masonry columns on barns are rounded to avoid cutting corner stones from such unworkable materials as slate. It is also worth remembering that buildings were sometimes disguised to look more expensive than they actually were. In the early nineteenth century, for example, it was popular to cover exterior brickwork or rubblework with a smooth stucco or to score it carefully with joints to imitate fine or rusticated stonework. Inside, plaster was scored to give the appearance of stone blocks, and softwood was 'grained' – painted to look like more expensive hardwoods.

Technology and trade also have an enormous impact on the development of our domestic spaces. Increased trade within Europe at the end of the seventeenth century, for example, brought about the importation of softwood from the Baltic, which heralded the switch from locally obtained hardwoods to pine for joinery, affecting both the design of mouldings and the size of panelling, which had to be painted to disguise the inferior pine. During the same period, on the eastern seaboard of the United States, luxury materials, such as marble used for mantelpieces, were imported from Europe along with more basic substances like slate. Brick,

ABOVE The mid-eighteenth-century principal staircase at Drayton Hall, near Charleston, South Carolina. The honey-coloured oak-turned balusters look striking against the intense blue panelling, which was last decorated in the nineteenth century.
OPPOSITE Detail of door.

OVERLEAF, CLOCKWISE FROM TOP LEFT Two panelled doors in Calke Abbey, Derbyshire have painted and grained finishes; the service area has yellow distemper walls and a rare mid-nineteenth-century Brussels carpet runner; another room at the abbey has its original 1860s wallpaper; time has gently faded the mid-nineteenth-century grey colour scheme in Drayton Hall, South Carolina.

pantiles and tin-glazed (or Delft) tiles were introduced more widely due to new links with the Netherlands. With mass production, improved transport (canals, railways, and roads) and urbanization came the adoption of new designs, technology, materials, trades and craftsmanship. Thus, by the mid-nineteenth century, materials such as bricks and slate became common in new towns and cities throughout the world.

Reflecting the changing lifestyles of families, social mores and domestic activities, house layouts have developed over time. Apart from the evolution of our basic human needs and interests, numerous other factors – such as context (town or countryside), technology and taste – were also influential. In the nineteenth century, for example, the refinement of the chimney, fireplace and grate as a separate decorative ensemble coincided with the social desire to receive guests in 'polite' reception rooms that were unsullied by the implements of mundane domestic chores. As a result, cooking moved away from the fireplace in living areas and into more sophisticated ranges in service rooms usually located at the rear of the house.

The shape of rooms also changed over time and according to new demands, a transition often signalled in different types of plaster under layers of wallpaper or cut-off cornices, indications of inserted partitions or new walls. As you try to re-imagine how the rooms in your house might have been originally used, look out for variations in plaster or wall coverings. Establishing whether a home is as it was first built or, as is often the case, a concatenation of various alterations and additions, reveals the ways in which the house has been used and might suggest ways of returning to the room's original functions while adapting them to modern living.

While the form and function of rooms have changed gradually over the centuries, design and decoration are inevitably tied to fashion, taste and innovation – fleeting features that can make creating an 'original' ambience difficult. After investigating the house's organization, architectural elements – mouldings, doors and window surrounds, architraves, fireplaces and staircases – can provide vital clues and dates to the house's construction and decoration. The sash window is a classic example: prior to its introduction in the late seventeenth century, windows were generally mullioned. By the eighteenth century, the sash had become the most fashionable window in northern Europe and North America, as well as in parts of Portugal, remaining popular to this day. It is still possible to date sash windows according to their features: early-eighteenth-century glazing bars were heavy in section, becoming more slender with time; with improvements in the manufacture of glass in the mid-nineteenth century, large sheets of glass began to overtake small-paned windows in popularity. During the same period, sash windows came to assume more decorative features, as in the carved 'horns' on the side timbers of the upper half of sash windows. Similarly, in the mouldings and panel layout, doors can hold clues to your house's history, but be warned that the twentieth-century desire for clean lines covered old panelled doors with sheets of hardboard to appear like flush doors.

Clues to the history of a house can be found everywhere, especially if you know where to look. Even details such as cast-iron grates (which in North America, for instance, remained popular from the mid-eighteenth century to the mid-nineteenth century before being superseded by arched register plate grates and later by grates with inset decorative tiles)

can offer tell-tale indications of a house's life. Perhaps the most difficult interior features to place are those that reflect a given period's fashion in design and material, particularly wall and floor coverings. Because taste is so ephemeral and because floor and wall surfaces are usually the first to be covered in a make-over, it is almost impossible to identify the initial surface. Careful and persistent excavation of walls and floors (which can have dozens of impenetrable layers of paint, paper, wood), particularly behind built-in cabinets or furniture, can often reveal a fascinating lineage of taste and trends, such as the vogue for painted pine panelling (popular in the late seventeenth century in the the United States, England and Ireland).

The well-worn interior offers a blueprint for retaining a unique and personal character and for respecting local building traditions and decorative styles of the past while accommodating a modern lifestyle and sensibility. Whether you decide to devote your whole home to the faded grandeur of yesteryear or to select only a few antiques to decorate an architect-designed modern interior, there are many lessons that can be learned from your house, whatever its age. The well-worn interior combines artful neglect, an appreciation of past traditions and technological advancement and a celebration of our daily changing lives.

living

marrying the historical with the contemporary

Old-fashioned comfort is slowly replacing the recent trend for minimal interiors. It is in these restful settings that we relax, take time out to think and enjoy moments of privacy, either alone or with friends and loved ones. We surround ourselves

with objects and decorations that reflect our inner selves, creating a personal bastion to protect ourselves from the outside world. Homey and lived-in, these are the special spaces where we feel completely at one with ourselves. The living area is where we indulge in the passions that fill our leisure time – collecting, reading, writing, painting or simply contemplating our lives.

ABOVE Detail of an early-nineteenth-century beechwood chair and its fine, original rush seat and painted faux-bamboo decoration.
LEFT The fragile beauty of these rare butterflies is exhibited in a late-nineteenth-century collection.
OPPOSITE Flaking distempered walls, scrubbed floorboards, worn rugs, framed engravings and personal memorabilia all have their unique place in a Dublin living room.

TOP Precious seventeenth-century Italian books luxuriously bound in cream vellum are housed in an unusual nineteenth-century bookcase with leather dust flaps attached to the shelves.
BOTTOM These beautiful eighteenth- and nineteenth-century French and English volumes are bound in leather and have delicate gilt tooling and coloured labels.
OPPOSITE The faded grey walls of this nineteenth-century study in East London are offset by the rich mahogany of the hall chair with its armorial coronet and the gilded French wall decoration.

What we today generally call a living room has throughout the history of houses had a variety of descriptions that reflect the room's use, period, custom and occupant's social standing. In cities, such rooms in the past were used for largely formal purposes – 'reception' rooms to withdraw to with esteemed guests. In rural areas, in contrast, living rooms were often combined with the kitchen; elsewhere, with a study, music room or, in a grander residence, museum-like spaces meant specifically to display the owner's taste for art or worldly travel.

Today, social formality is less prevalent, we tend to see our dwellings as places to relax away from the modern world. In a technology-driven global culture, the television – or, increasingly, the computer – has become the focal point of the living space, which has adapted, often taking in the strewn objects of family life or even a home office. But lifestyles have always changed, and our living spaces have evolved to accommodate those changes. Although some of these transformations might seem antithetical to older houses, the modern accoutrements of contemporary homes can often enhance and diversify the quality of the time-worn interior, and nowhere is the felicitous combination of old and new, of modern and contemporary so possible as in the living room.

Since the very beginnings of our human dwellings, the fireplace has been at the heart of living space. As our habitations developed, what was once a means of survival through heat and cooking assumed importance as a strong decorative element: the hearth became the place to stack logs and keep coal scuttles, fire irons and fireguards; the mantelpiece, itself often an object of decoration, was used to display family photographs, invitations, visiting cards and old portrait miniatures. Modern living requirements and central heating systems may have eradicated the need for fireplaces, which has led to such elements being blocked or removed, but the appeal of a flickering fire is timeless.

Another aspect of the living room that is independent of place and time is the need to sit, to lounge, to relax, to converse. Streamlined designer furniture may be pleasing to some, but lush deep upholstered seats are undeniably vital to encourage guests to gather around the hearth in winter, to stimulate an intimate conversation or to fall into after a hectic day. Unlike metal-legged, foam-rubbered design statements that *look* great, old worn sofas *feel* great, and act as tempting day beds, inviting moments of respite from the day's chores. Blankets, shabby shawls or stunning pieces of antique textiles can be draped – even thrown on in layers – or placed strategically to hide patches of threadbare velvet covers or faded chintz.

While seating might be the room's most inviting element, it is worth considering the important function of tables. With its piles of newspapers, ashtrays and everyday miscellanea, the modern coffee table has its origins in the tea table, a more elegant and delicate object than its present-day equivalent. Small and usually circular or oblong, the tea table was supported on a tripod stand and intended for easy mobility – a very modern aspect. When not in use, its hinged tops could be swung vertical and the table placed against the wall. Just as the coffee table does today, it could be used to hold alternatives sources of light, a lamp or candle.

While the table can be used for a variety of functions, including display, shelving for display and storage can provide essential space for books, DVDs or objects that are the focus of a collecting passion. The craze for collecting (see p. 168) reached its zenith in the nineteenth century, a period that saw custom-built glass-fronted cases exhibit everything from shells and butterflies to fine china; many became personal museums or cabinets of curiosity.

The contemporary living room has a wonderful array of uses and contents. Today, our personal collections may stand side by side with our library, office or study; well-thumbed books line shelves or bookcases and writing desks are stuffed with old letters and littered with boxes of personal ephemera, or indeed newer items, such as electronic gadgets or digital photographs. The space may also be our music room – here we listen to our hi-fi. A violin might hang on the wall, an old record player or gramophone may stand in the corner.

The beauty of the time-worn room, whatever the particular components it might contain, is the manner in which it can accommodate an eclectic mix of objects, furniture , moods or uses. Artfully composed, the antiquated and the modern can combine to create a romantic, used and loved interior.

The grey-painted panelling in this high-ceilinged room in a French château near Vichy dates from the mid-eighteenth century. The mighty white-marble fireplace and stylish oak chevron parquet floor, an especially popular pattern in France, create a stunning geometric effect, against which the owners can best enjoy the simplicity of a roaring fire. It is important to remember that the well-worn interior often looks the most visually pleasing when simple furnishings are complemented by one or two striking details.

In this palatial Italian drawing room, in a nineteenth-century castello near Turin, the window recess has become a favourite reading spot and a comfortable position from which to gaze out over the rooftops and baroque church beneath. The painted shutters are decorated in early-twentieth-century trompe l'oeils. Specialists in this type of decoration are found internationally and can help to create a unique environment in the living area.

above In the corner of a New York apartment sits a handsome early-nineteenth-century French Empire writing desk. The elegantly symmetrical design draws the eye to the piece's sleek curves and considered details. Working at this beautifully crafted object and making use of the series of cubbyholes and hidden drawers brings moments of undeniable pleasure to the user, even when writing out bills!

'On leaving his love, the focus of a man's reflections is in large part the pretty inanimate objects which his passion has invested with a little of the nature and character of his love.'

Edmond de Goncourt, *La maison d'un artiste*

clockwise, from top left A correspondence box contains fading handwritten old letters tied with pink silk ribbons, and a personal history revealed in diaries from 1860 and 1883; the deceptively restrained and simple design of this early-nineteenth-century German Biedermeier writing cabinet conceals a series of secret compartments; a rather romantic notion, this mid-eighteenth-century English case was used to carry treasured letters when travelling and is lined with pages from books; Scottish cabinet-making at its best – this square piano of 1816 has a veneered satinwood interior cross-banded with rosewood and painted with the makers name (Alexander Knowles of Aberdeen).

opposite, clockwise from top left Exquisite wood-block illustrations in a vellum-bound Spanish book of proverbs (1733), which invites the visitor to flick through the pages; a veined marble mantelpiece is home to a shrine with rococo porcelain candlesticks and a majolica Madonna in an Italian palazzo; what secrets are held in this nineteenth-century correspondence resting on the green baize of an English writing table?; delightful nineteenth-century watercolour box still showing its maker's intense blue label; decorative nineteenth-century French cast of an Ionic column; sink into this reading chair upholstered in original blue French rococo cotton (c. 1860).

above Years of loving use have romantically softened and frayed the early-nineteenth-century printed toile-cotton upholstery on an eighteenth-century gilded armchair in the French style. Certain establishments nowadays allow you to design your own fabric patterns or can re-create your favourite designs. The grand piano is seductively shabby and several missing ivory keys suggest a long and colourful history far outdating its present home in an Irish country house.

left A first-floor parlour in an early-eighteenth-century silkweaver's house in London has unevenly sized scrubbed deal floorboards and late-eighteenth-century decoration. The painted panelling on the walls has a grey border, which is intended to give the illusion of fielding (the chamfered edging to panelling). An early-nineteenth-century elm tea table and country Hepplewhite chair furnish the room. The placement and type of furniture makes a big impact on a room's atmosphere. Here, in spite of very faded décor, the living area still retains a formal air due to the style and positioning of the furniture. Visitors are enticed to move deeper into the house when they catch glimpses of other rooms through the open doors.

below A deeply buttoned mid-nineteenth-century Victorian Irish reading chair sits by a fine marble fireplace in a Dublin townhouse.

left Deep-red, floor-to-ceiling silk curtains with
a subtly patterned trim are sure to shut out dark
evenings in this Italian castello. Using such
textiles as velvet or silk will always bring a touch
of luxury to a room. A painted bergère chair is
carefully placed to benefit from the natural light
that enters the room. Textures are also an
important consideration in a room's composition:
the light catches the rough material of the cane
chair, which is counter-balanced by the sweeping
softness of the curtains.

above The popularity of this handsome William
IV Irish mahogany sofa is evident with its
craquelure (cracked finish) cover hiding the straw
pallet. Velvet cushions add extra comfort, and the
flower motif carved on the back of the sofa is
echoed on the chairs against the wall to create
a sense of unity in the room. These kinds of
attention to detail will not go unnoticed by the
observant guest.

27 living

left Sixteenth-century oak panelling sets off
the frayed crimson velvet sofa with its gilded
braid in the great parlour of a Shropshire
manor house. The braid and fringing give the
sofa an even more faded grandeur and are
details that could be sewn onto any sofa. With
hinged arms, the sofa can be transformed into a
relaxing day bed or provide more seating
arrangements for social gatherings. An early
Georgian ancestor in complementary red dress
peeps around the corner of the sofa.

below A small Italian waxen madonna draped
with beads and silk sits in a Dutch seventeenth-
century ebonized frame. This haunting image
is found in the living room of a German
apartment in East Berlin.

left to right A wood-panelled Dublin study is home
to a mid-nineteenth-century, mahogany and green-
leather library chair. An early-nineteenth-century
Greek-revival armchair has deep relief carving on
the legs, arms and back. The yellow of the seat is an
attractive contrast to the dark wood frame. The blue
satin on the seat of this smart gilded mahogany
Italian chair complements the floor tiles. Notice how
the style, colours and decoration on each chair have
been thought through to ensure that it fits
seamlessly into its surroundings, evoking the right
atmosphere for the room's purpose: for example, the
gilded chair standing on the smart floor tiles exudes
a more formal air than the effect of contrasting
wood and leather.

opposite Reminiscent of the colour of old cinema
seats, the intense hue of the red velvet covers on this
1930s armchair is brought out by the backdrop of
sober French grey panelling.

31 living

above An invitingly well-worn French toffee-coloured leather armchair is pulled up to an early-nineteenth-century cast-iron grate in Spitalfields, London. A tea table is within easy reach, and the candle casts its light over the reader's shoulder and illuminates the old dial telephone. In fact, not only has everything in this vista been positioned practically for the fireside lounger, but it also guarantees his comfort.

opposite Panelling painted a chocolate brown, pine floorboards swathed in oriental rugs and a pair of Hogarth engravings create an intimate environment in this Georgian house in East London. A favourite collection of mugs are allocated a prominent position above the tiny regency fireplace.

'The interior represents the universe for the private individual.

He collects there whatever is distant, whatever is of the past.

His living room is a box in the theatre of the world.'

Walter Benjamin, *Schriften*, 'Louis-Philippe oder der Interieur', 1955

A nineteenth-century plush red armchair and bright striped French cushion cover heighten the snugness around this early-eighteenth-century hearthside in London. If you are unable to find antique pieces of cloth, contemporary materials often come in very similar patterns; if trying to re-create this look, select natural fibres rather than synthetic textiles. The English blue Delft tiles of the fire surround depict biblical scenes and were made in the 1720s. The tongs, poker and shovel and the barely cold ashes are a reminder that the fireplace is used regularly.

opposite The focal point of this room in Derbyshire is the wall decoration: watercolours, texts and natural-history specimens on a background of nineteenth-century blue wallpaper. Frames range from the lavishly ornate to the simpler bird's-eye-maple designs. Framing can be a costly operation, and it is sometimes worth scouring secondhand shops – pictures can easily be changed and you may find an antique frame. It would appear that the owner is an avid collector of personal memorabilia – maybe an ancestor takes pride of place?

'The collection of curiosities … were agreeably dispersed among small specimens of china and glass, various neat trifles made by the proprietor of the museum, and some tobacco-stoppers carved by the Aged.'

Charles Dickens, *Great Expectations*, 1860

left The mid-nineteenth-century Bird Lobby at Calke Abbey, Derbyshire is testament to Sir Vauncey Harpur Crewe's collecting bug. Glass display cases show all manner of winged creatures from around the world, some of which are now extinct. An unusual form of wall decoration, but one that can easily be used today.

right Shiny shells and differently coloured minerals look fabulous in the pull-out trays of this wonderful early-nineteenth-century purpose-made cabinet in the Gothic style. Collection and ornamentation in one.

left The doors in this top-floor study in a London townhouse have rather remarkably retained their nineteenth-century paintwork. A miscellaneous arrangement of coral, feathers, shells and a statue of a Hindu god all remind the owner of overseas journeys, while an old pewter tankard holds sunflowers from the garden. right An old sash window has been recycled as internal glazing, a fairly inexpensive alteration and one which affords extra light in and a view upstairs from a small living chamber in Whitechapel, London. A French country Empire longcase clock chimes the hour and draws the reader, lost in an imaginary world, back to reality. On the bookcase rests a bronzed bust and a Biedermeier birch box.

entertaining
the social mise en scène

The functions of living and entertaining rooms have always overlapped, never more so than today. Although forms of entertainment have changed, it is human nature to derive pleasure from performance and communal activities.

Our time for diversion is precious, so it is important that our social interactions be uplifting, inspiring and unpredictable, entertainments in which we can participate. The space in which we choose to hold these gatherings must be considered carefully to create a stimulating and welcoming environment.

OPPOSITE Double mahogany doors are pushed open to reveal the drawing room of a Dublin townhouse. A gilded rococo mirror sits majestically above the mantelpiece, and it seems like the seat at the rosewood piano has just been vacated.
LEFT An early-nineteenth-century miniature.
ABOVE Toy theatres often provided an evening's entertainment; this particular one is a Dutch model.

Throughout Europe and the United States, small houses in the eighteenth, nineteenth and early twentieth century had a smart room used to receive and entertain guests, usually reserved for Sundays, holidays and for important family or social events. In grander establishments, this often meant an elegant drawing room or music room and in the homes of the very wealthy a saloon or even a ballroom. All kinds of activities happened here – music, dancing, singing and amateur dramatics – intended to captivate the guests.

Although the entertainment room was often the destination for visitors, the entrance area was where guests caught their first glimpse of things to come – a pillared marble hall perhaps, or a simple lobby in a humble cottage – the place visitors would wait before being ushered into receiving apartments or reception rooms. As the first public space, the entrance hall, with its architectural and formal decoration, functioned as a kind of pre-performance space; architectural theatre before live performance.

The spaces for entertaining had all available money, resources and craftsmanship lavished upon them. This was the room in which to use luxurious materials – real mahogany for doors, for example, solid marble for fireplace surrounds and the finest steel or cast-iron for fire grates. Even the soft furnishings reflected the desire to impress: the finest exotic carpets were laid on the floors and in the smartest establishments walls were hung with silk. Opulent fabrics were sewn into curtains and

used to upholster furniture. In the homes of the truly privileged, mirrors, curtain pelmets and often furniture were gilded; portraits of family members and important connections hung on the walls. In some places, especially Italy, for example, walls were decorated with paintings and frescoes to portray the theme of entertainment – musical instruments, food, drink, classical columns, statuary, idealized landscapes and Greek and Roman gods all created a bacchanalian backdrop to the festivities.

Once received and duly impressed, guests had to be accommodated, refreshed and put at ease. Smart settees and chairs were provided, and if the main body of the room needed to be clear for dancing, seats were arranged against the wall with their backs touching the dado rail. Refreshments played an essential role in this room, and elaborate dumb waiters – a small lift on pulleys set into the wall – transported consumables from the kitchen and butler's pantry to the entertaining room. In less technologically advanced homes, a tray or, more usefully, a butler's tray (a mahogany high-sided tray with a purpose-made hinged stand) sufficed. Tea was often stored in these rooms in a lockable caddy.

With the dual role of acting as a piece of furniture and the focus of a performance, a piano was an important centrepiece for the space. Supported on brass castors, it could be moved to the required position in the room according to the level of performance, whether for an intimate evening soirée or a more formal chamber arrangement. Similarly, as large, furniture-size pieces, billiard or pool tables could provide the focal point for entertainment in the form of games.

Today, perhaps because performances tend to take place in large public venues rather than in the residences of the privileged classes, entertainment spaces are often incorporated in the central living areas – but this is no excuse for not drawing out the qualities of such spaces to make them conducive to music, dancing or gaming. What we can learn from the grand and less grand entertainment rooms of the past is a sense of occasion, a modicum of formality for those social events in which activityless, informal lounging is almost universal.

RIGHT Yellow ochre-washed walls in the vaulted family billiard room of a hilltop castello near Turin.
OPPOSITE, TOP TO BOTTOM Furniture has been set back to the wall for dancing in this mid-nineteenth-century drawing room in a planter's house, Charleston, South Carolina; view through into the drawing room of a mid-nineteenth-century Italian palazzo; double doors open into this Dublin townhouse's entertaining room.

opposite The late-Georgian sofa, covered in wonderfully faded, ginger-coloured velvet, is set back to the wall in the Red Drawing Room of Castletown House near Dublin. Note the style of the sofa with its upright back and very few cushions – unlike in the living area, the visitor is encouraged to sit up straight in the entertaining rooms. The eighteenth-century manner of placing furniture against the wall allows the room to fill with guests and creates a more formal environment.

above left The fine Carrera marble mantel shelf is edged with a gilded fillet and stands out boldly from the wallpaper, which, despite its rips and tears, still manages to create a sense of grandeur in this room.

above right The processional route from one sumptuous interior to another, allowing a view along the length of the house.

'The houses are always clean and well kept … and they are always careful to keep one small sitting room spotlessly clean and sometimes quite elegant. In this room they receive their guests; the tables and chairs contained in it are of well polished mahogany, the chimney-piece is sometimes marble but generally of carved wood.'

François de la Rochefoucauld, 1784

below At the head of the principal staircase
of this eighteenth-century Dublin townhouse,
visitors are greeted by a triumphal arch washed
with old red distemper before being ushered
into the rooms prepared for their entertainment.
It is important to remember that a room
does not need many furnishings to make a
striking statement.

right A lone deeply buttoned banquette is
reflected in a large gilded looking-glass in an
ante-bellum house in Charleston, South Carolina.
It is many a year since this first-floor salon has seen
dancing, although its peeling wallpaper
and chipped gilt still evokes a sense of occasion.

opposite Trompe l'oeils play a big role in the decoration of the entertaining areas in this palazzo in northern Italy. Idealized classical landscapes, busts of Roman emperors and urns adorn the walls and create a good talking point. Areas missing paint and scenes that have become slightly blurred suggest that many a guest has run their hand admiringly along the painted decoration.

right Classical architraves, a grotesque head and paper bills pasted to a boarded doorway with glimpses of azure sky beyond: all is an illusion. In fact, you are looking at the finest trompe l'oeils on a canvas backing in the 'grotto room' of a Victorian row house in New York City. The trompe-l'oeil technique is still practised widely by skilled craftsmen and makes a stunning alternative to a painting or tapestry, adding the illusion of space and depth to a room.

SALTATE MVSICA TEMPORIS

'Have nothing in your houses you do not know to be useful or believe to be beautiful.'
William Morris quoted in *Chapters in Workshop Reconstruction and Citizenship* by C. R. Ashbee, 1894

opposite Evenings of musical entertainment can be enjoyed by every generation, and it is easy to envisage a gathering of folk around the piano to celebrate a special occasion or to simply round off a pleasurable evening by indulging in that feel-good pastime of singing. In this Irish drawing room, the grand piano rests on uneven floorboards, while a threadbare Turkey rug marks clearly the division between performer and spectator.

right An elegant, nineteenth-century Broadwood square piano sits against a panelled wall in this London home, but a cleverly placed mirror keeps the pianist in touch with what is going on in the room behind.

'The evening came, the drawing-rooms were lighted up, the company assembled. It was but a card-party, it was but a mixture of those who had never met before, and those who met too often – a common-place business, too numerous for intimacy, too small for variety; but Anne had never found an evening shorter.'

Jane Austen, *Persuasion*, 1818

left Another example of a square piano, here in a heavier style, appears in a Dublin townhouse; the instrument's dark rosewood is striking against the arsenic green walls. The sheets of music look as if they have been extensively thumbed through over the years, while the formal picture hang of mezzotints helps to create an air of elegant entertainment.

above Until the end of the eighteenth century, tea was served in bowls while coffee was drunk from a handled can. Now, too precious to use for entertaining, this gilded regency Coalport tea bowl and coffee can are displayed on the mantelpiece in a late-eighteenth-century sea captain's house in London. Pieces of china, whether antique or contemporary, are a traditional form of decoration on the mantel-piece. They flank a black-framed miniature of an East Anglian farmer in profile.

clockwise from top left It has been customary for many centuries to hang pictures of ancestors or immediate family on the walls of the more ceremonial rooms, and this look can easily be adopted in any home, whether with 'real' ancestors or not. A pressed paper profile in a typical early-nineteenth-century English miniature frame; a miniature of an early-nineteenth-century English gentleman farmer; a haunting self-portrait of the artist in a classical setting; an eighteenth-century English Northumbrian squire.

opposite This corner of an Irish country house has a robust regency mahogany sideboard that holds an extensive drinks selection, an essential component of any entertainment area. Dining chairs in the style of Sheraton and a tiered dumbwaiter table are nearby. The decorative frieze above the door is composed of plaster. Today, as a last resort and if you are unable to find original plasterwork, moulds can be bought in most DIY or art shops.

opposite Afternoon tea is served by a log fire in this late-Georgian townhouse in London; a crisp white damask tablecloth and napkin contrast with the fatigued wooden floor.

right An internal sash window, inserted by the present owner, is an excellent way of allowing light to penetrate deep into the drawing room. When entertaining large numbers of people, this is a simple way of keeping the party united even when guests are spread between rooms.

below A brightly coloured, early Staffordshire (c. 1800) figure shows Diana the huntress reaching for an arrow from her quiver.

left Dusty-blue walls offset by opulent gilding decorate the principal entertaining room of the Aitken-Rhett house in Charleston, South Carolina. This mansion in the deep south, built before the American Civil War, has retained its mid-nineteenth-century decoration redolent of a past way of life with its marble fireplace and gilt mirror. Candles used to be the only lighting available at night, but even today they bring a magical light to any room.

right The entertainment chamber in a Dublin townhouse is glimpsed from behind a rich mahogany door with a wonderful figured grain. The banquette sofas now show the results of years of heavy partying, but still tempt guests engrossed in conversation to slump down under the impressive early-nineteenth-century family portrait. Banquettes, such as these, are good space-saving seating in rooms intended to hold many guests.

left What better wall decoration for a room intended to host evenings of entertainment among friends than paintings that transport guests to the glories of an ancient time? The odd floor tile is missing, reminding visitors that they do not have to stand on ceremony in this Italian palazzo.

right, clockwise from top left Decoration is an integral part in fostering a party atmosphere. A close-up of the dumbwaiter reveals that it is cleverly disguised as a gilded cage in which two exotic birds perch – what a superb way of hiding the often unsightly hatches between kitchen and dining areas in the more modern home; faded by two-hundred years of sunlight, this print room near Dublin still retains the elegance it had when first created for entertaining; detail of a copper-plate engraving of figures from classical antiquity, which are framed by printed paper borders and decorated with festoons of ribbons; the colourful scrap screen enlivens an Irish drawing room, which is used for intimate and relaxed gatherings. Compiling your own scrap screen could not be simpler, and it can be decorated to reflect individual taste, be it with pictures of loved ones, mementos from trips abroad or personal memorabilia.

cooking and eating

age-old essentials

Since time immemorial, the kitchen-cum-eating area is the home's heart, the space where we derive pleasure from mouth-watering menus composed from the freshest ingredients and where we enjoy the company of friends

and family enlivened by the preparation and enjoyment of food. Usually the most frequently used room in the house, the kitchen is often the quickest to become ravaged by time. So many of the appealing characteristics of the faded kitchen have been lost in the world of stainless-steel appliances and ready-made cabinetry. However functional our kitchen may now be, we must not forget those early morning chats or late-night intimacies that can be shared around a stove casting a glow on the fading limewash or the worn work surfaces.

OPPOSITE Limewashed walls, pine shelves and iron hooks are found in an old pantry at Calke Abbey, Derbyshire.
LEFT A delightful nineteenth-century hanging candle box is still coated in its original pillar-box red paint.
ABOVE A pestle and mortar, garden twine and a flour sieve each have their own compartment on the kitchen shelves of a London town house in Whitechapel.

Up until the eighteenth century, the kitchen was generally located away from the central residence as a fire precaution, and cooking remained an activity that was combined with other daytime occupations. In an old farmhouse or cottage, the room with the largest fireplace opening was often the living kitchen, or what we would now use as the living room. As time progressed, cooking and preparation was fully incorporated into a house's functions, usually in the service areas of wealthy and middle-class homes. In the grandest establishments, entrance to the working areas was through a baize door hung on pivots to ease the journey of many maids with full trays. It also acted as a sound barrier, keeping the bustle and noise of the kitchen away from the rest of the house. Townhouses often had kitchens in the cellar or in a rear wing. Thus, it is only in recent years that we have rediscovered the relatively informal arrangement of the kitchen as a cooking and eating area.

Although the cooking range is central to culinary operations, its functions other than preparing food have been lost. Before the advent of modern heating systems, the cooker heated water for washing and the room was kept warm with its open fire. Until the cooking range was introduced in the late eighteenth century, large fireplaces (with an assortment of ironwork, including firedogs, spits for turning meat and pot hooks) were used for cooking, while a brick, stone or clay oven was often used for baking.

At first, cooking ranges were basic, with an iron basket (often a collection of horizontal iron bars) high above the hearth, set between stone or iron shelves (hobs), on which pans and kettles could be rested. By the mid-nineteenth century, cast-iron ranges were more common, with either an open fire basket or a closed fire box covered by an iron plate. Later in the same century, doors adorned with ceramic tiles were placed within the cast-iron framework, a tradition that survived into the era of enamelled

metal, which became fashionable for ranges during the 1920s.

The nineteenth century also saw significant advancements in services, developments that we take for granted today – water provision was improved; lighting (initially gas, later electricity) was introduced; and floor coverings, such as linoleum, were invented. Sculleries adjacent to the kitchen became a regular feature, where food was prepared, and a piped water supply meant that it could double up as a washhouse. Depending on the local materials, sinks came in a variety of materials – stone, lead-lined timber and salt-glazed or white earthenware. They were generally supported on brick or stone piers, cast-iron legs or set into a timber worktop within a cupboard.

Storage is and always will be of vital importance in this area of the house, serving both practical and decorative needs. In most houses, cupboards, the smartest ones having curved decorative shelf fronts, go a long way

toward fulfilling this function. Corner cupboards or glazed doors with shelves behind and the dresser with wall rack above were common features and an opportunity for ornamented painted surfaces or woodwork. French cupboard doors, for example, are rarely solid, having wire netting to protect the goods within.

In the perennial quest for efficiency in our contemporary houses, we find the time for cooking and food preparation more precious, so we are increasingly seduced by the sleek fitted kitchen with granite work surfaces, stainless steel and hardwood fittings. Signalling a return of the kitchen to the house's focal point, the farmhouse kitchen – whether in the city or the country – has gained popularity in style and function and re-presents a wealth of design and decorative ideas that had been lost over time. Sturdy furniture and a prominent fireplace or stove with an assortment of pans and utensils help give us a sense of security, homeliness and comfort. Rustic woods, like oak, can be left in their raw state, unlike softwoods, like pine, which usually need to be painted. However modern our requirements for cooking and eating may have become, our basic need for down-to-earth home comforts and the value of natural ingredients and materials will never fade.

RIGHT A sturdy coal-burning stove masterfully sits in the kitchen of a former Irish schoolhouse. The owner uses the hotplates to dry orange peel and other consumables.
OPPOSITE, LEFT TO RIGHT The green baize door separates above and below stairs. A workaday pine kitchen table with scrubbed sycamore top still has its original turquoise paint. An English Delft plate sits next to a Cumbrian brown slip-glazed jug in an East London kitchen.

left Varying hues and finishes of wood, in the
form of panelling, floorboards, furniture and
shelving, dominate the layout of this housekeeper's
room in London. Different shades of the same
colour always liven up a room and create the need
for less ornamentation. China adds a more delicate
element to the space and is displayed in an
eighteenth-century fitted cupboard with
curved shelf fronts. The unusual position of
the mirror injects a fresh perspective into the
room. The hearth is a wonderful pattern of old
rubbed-down tiles.

below Small details bring a wealth of character
and flavour to a room. These well-used early-
nineteenth-century japanned and gilded tea tins
from a coffee and tea merchant's shop transport
the room back to the 1800s, whilst still providing
handy modern-day storage containers. Chinese
lettering adorns one caddy, while the other is
labelled as the merchant's tea number eleven.

above A mahogany butler's tray is laden with cutlery and crockery to take above stairs. It is interesting to note that these simple cutlery designs have a timeless quality about them. The novelty of naturalistic design is evident in the cabbage-leaf majolica dessert plates.
opposite Creating a distinctly Dickensian atmosphere, this panelled dining room can actually be found in a silkweaver's house in modern-day London. Simple pewter and Delft plates indicate a supper without company.

'The laying out of a table must greatly depend upon the nature of the dinner or supper, the taste of the host, the description of the company, and the appliances possessed.… The whiteness of the table-cloth, the clearness of glass, the polish of plate, and the judicious distribution of ornamental groups of fruits and flowers, are matters deserving the utmost attention.'

Enquire Within Upon Everything, published by Houlston and Sons, 1887

left Storage units are often the most visible aspects of the kitchen, allowing the creative cook to introduce colour, texture and variety to the space. Here, a glass and wood kitchen cupboard has been hung on the nailed-down panelled walls of a Spitalfields' kitchen in London.

right An old French free-standing china cupboard stands in an otherwise minimalist kitchen; its glazed display section, small cutlery drawer and distressed wood finish adds character to the room.

clockwise, from top left The use of colour is an important element in these cupboards for both utilitarian and visual purposes. Peacock-blue woodwork was a favourite shade for cupboard interiors, and, as shown here, provides a pleasing backdrop to the pieces kept within the eighteenth-century bow-fronted English corner cupboard. From a more practical perspective, the 'dolly' blue limewash of the fitted china cupboard is intended to repel flies. Finally, exquisite Chinese export porcelain is displayed on purpose-built decorative shelves. opposite Gone are the days when every cooking area had an open fire, but this basement kitchen in a sea captain's house in London still keeps the tradition alive and functional. The flagstone floor, cast-iron cooking range, fitted and corner cupboards and dresser make this interior feel cosy and lived in.

below The shapes and positions of sinks have changed dramatically over the centuries to accommodate the cook's requirements. This timber sink at Calke Abbey in Derbyshire is lined with lead, which is soft and pliable, to minimize breakages. The chipped stone walls, splintering wood surround and single, slightly skewed tap makes us think of an era long passed when cold water was the only option.

opposite Continuing the almost medieval theme, the crumbling, vaulted stone kitchen of a French château near Clermont-Ferrand has a wide and functional stone sink with a bronze tap attached high above the basin. The key to this space, seemingly hollowed from a slab of rock, is that it has been left untouched and unmodernized through the centuries, stoically withstanding the test of time.

pages 76–77 Clearly divided between the preparation space and the eating area, this cavernous French kitchen-cum-dining-room has much rustic charm. Unafraid of clutter, this cook likes to be able to cast her eye over the kitchen's contents without having to root around in cupboards. A superb example of the pleasing balance of old – clay floor tiles, centuries-old limeplastered walls that have never seen a lick of paint, original doors – and new – all manner of modern kitchen utensils, a music system, an impressive cooker – without losing the appeal of either.

left Back to basics: the hand-turned elm bowl
containing fresh artichokes brings a taste of the
country into this farmhouse in Virginia, USA.
right Nineteenth-century, green majolica dessert
plates continue the appreciation of nature and
complement the bare wooden surface.
opposite Mix and match the styles of chairs
around the dining table to create an informal
and well-worn atmosphere, heightened, here,
by the scrubbed pine table top and well-
trodden flagstones.

pages 80–81, clockwise, from left
An iron pot stand holds an assortment of old
kitchen equipment: a carved marble mortar,
an enamelled pan dating from the 1930s and
an American, black-glazed mixing bowl. It is
interesting to note that older saucepans have
longer handles, leaving the tops of the handles
cooler to the touch in an age when heat-resistant
materials did not exist. To create an authentic
evocation of a past age does not mean that items
of furniture need be restricted to the room for
which they were originally intended; this late-
eighteenth-century English ladder-back chair with
rush seat was probably meant for outdoor use in
a summerhouse, but functions equally as well now

as a chair around the kitchen table. Aside from the
vivid shades of blue that decorate these kitchen
walls, a room's fixtures and fittings offer important
clues as to the mood the owner is trying to create.
A ceramic Belfast sink with a battered lead
splashback and old brass taps, vegetables in the
sink ready to be prepared and a pigeon waiting
to be plucked, all indicate that a lot of time is spent
in this London kitchen. A modern wall-mounted
dish drainer is a very practical addition to this
composition and one which does not look out of
place. Images of candlelit evenings of merriment
are conjured up by these half-full, nineteenth-
century wine glasses and fine, George III,
cut-glass decanter.

opposite Let your imagination take over – adapt and convert pieces of furniture to suit your needs. Employed here as kitchen shelves, this storage system was originally a set of drawers from an early-nineteenth-century London chemist's shop. Traces of the original painted name labels still remain on the rough and distressed surfaces. Various spices and seasonings are kept in glass preserving jars.

clockwise, from top left Perhaps a trophy from a hunting trip, this bear is now a fearsome reminder to remove your hat before eating in this Dublin kitchen; a polished kettle sits atop an old cream-coloured Aga, behind which are spice drawers and a sycamore pastry board; open shutters in a London basement allow light to fall onto a scrubbed pine table top, where a French cheese cover and English fruitwood tea caddy are laid out for a light meal; a gently decaying painted highchair has a resting place in the kitchen of a French farmhouse near Clermont-Ferrand.

'The room itself was large though low; and the heavy frames of its old
fashioned windows, and the heavy beams in its crooked ceiling, seemed
to indicate that it had once been a house of some mark standing alone
in the country.'

Charles Dickens, *Our Mutual Friend*, 1878

left Yellow ochre walls and basic, painted pine
furniture make up this old kitchen in central
England. The room is lit by windows placed high
up in the wall to prevent those toiling below from
becoming distracted by outside events.
right An elegant pantry in a château near Vichy,
France is painted in grey. Fine wire mesh, as
opposed to solid door panels, allows good
ventilation around the cupboard's contents, an
effect that is easily achievable on more modern
kitchen cabinets. Old scales can often be found in
antique shops and make a useful and attractive
piece of kitchen equipment.
opposite It looks as if huge vats of stew have been
left bubbling away unattended on the gargantuan
cast-iron cooking range in an old kitchen in
Derbyshire. The shabby surroundings have a soft
melancholy about them.

The kitchen, with the kettle on the hob, looks warm and comfortable from the entrance hall of this eighteenth-century house in Spitalfields, London. Exposed brickwork and the spearmint and buff paintwork bring a serenity to the composition. Tea towels hang drying by the Aga and the slate work surfaces are washed down; all is arranged in an orderly fashion. If you have plasterboard walls in an old house, it is often advisable to investigate what is behind them – you might uncover some old brickwork that is much more attractive.

sleeping

peaceful havens away from modern-day bustle

The bedroom is the inner sanctum, the home's most private space, not just an area for sleeping but for unwinding and relaxing. It was only a century ago that it was common for children or indeed whole families to share a bed, but for most

people today separate bedrooms have become a necessary part of our domestic arrangements. There is no escaping the need for sleep, so the bedroom has become a refuge from the trials and tribulations of the day. Whether it contains an ascetic purity or a cluttered cosiness, the bedroom is our escape from the world.

OPPOSITE Seen through the doorway, this monastic-style bedroom in the tower of a château in the Auvergne, France has an early-twentieth-century brass bed.
LEFT A bedside table has a French alarm clock and an early-nineteenth-century English tortoiseshell case for visiting cards.
ABOVE French ticking on a mattress.

BELOW An Irish four-poster has elaborate nineteenth-century hangings and two steps to make access easier.
OPPOSITE A bedroom in an Italian castello near Turin has hand-blocked early-nineteenth-century French wallpaper, portraying classical figures in a Claudian landscape.

In many homes of the medieval period in Europe, occupants slept around a fire in the open hall or in lofts above other rooms. Only the master of the house had private sleeping quarters. By the seventeenth century, medium-sized farmhouses had private sleeping rooms, often on the ground floor, while farmhands and children slept upstairs in the loft. Bedrooms or bedchambers were gradually incorporated in all but the poorest homes. The wealthy had private apartments in their houses, which included a living area, dressing room, private closet and bedchamber, much in the manner of a modern self-contained apartment. By the late seventeenth century, the urban middle classes also had bedchambers on the upper floors of their townhouses. Aside from in the single-storey cottage or bungalow, the position of the bedroom above the central living areas has remained the most common location. Cold houses and draughty rooms have always meant that the protection and comfort of the occupants from the elements is of utmost importance in the bedroom, which remains a primary consideration today.

The most immediate – and, as it developed, the most elaborate – means of cocooning oneself took its form in a canopied or four-poster bed, which provided its own roomlike environment. Sixteenth- and seventeenth-century beds with turned oak posts, panelled backs and canopies gave way to ornate upholstered baroque beds hung with richly coloured damasks and velvets.

Later, in the eighteenth century, the neoclassical style inspired lighter designs with turned and carved mahogany posts and printed cottons and chintzes. Decoration was influenced by local design and motifs as well as international fashion: in the United States, for example, bed posts were carved with rice leaves and in Scandinavia the tradition of painted furniture meant foliage, figures and text adorned bedsteads.

Although it was common to have bedsteads with no more than a head and base board or rail, canopied beds were also found in simpler homes. Beds in Irish cottages and farmhouses often had boards at their foot and head, with an arched top. This idea of enclosure took another form throughout northern Europe, where beds were located in cupboards near the main fireplace.

Suggesting perhaps that when we sleep we desire a return to older times, old beds – albeit upgraded with spring mattresses – are more popular than ever today. Such is our desire for the safe and protective qualities of old beds that reproductions are made in large quantities (the details of which are not always true to the original design), and in recent years, French bateau beds and the four-poster have returned to favour.

Throughout its history, the need to make a soft, womblike environment has meant the bedroom provides the most opportunity for textiles and soft furnishings, whether in bed coverings, draperies, pillow or cushion covers. From quilts, sheets and pillowcases to throws and hangings, most comfort fabrics achieve their highest state of refinement in the bedroom. In recent years, the laborious patchwork quilt, for example, seems to have a new-found appeal.

All these fabrics and bed linens, not to mention clothing, create a need for a substantial amount of storage in the bedroom. As in the house's other rooms, the needs and use of storage has developed over centuries. Until the seventeenth century, for instance, clothes were hung on wooden pegs in a bedroom, or folded in a chest; only some grander households had closets for clothes. By the nineteenth century, many small houses had walk-in closets. Our modern wardrobes have evolved from the closet, and throughout Europe local traditions and taste have influenced the style of these pieces. The Dutch, for example, have very fine seventeenth-century pieces decorated with ebonized wood, prominent cornices and resting on turned ball feet. Throughout the world there have been variations on freestanding bed linen storage, from elaborate chest of drawers to assortments of cupboards, from commodes to presses (a cupboard for hanging clothes with a set of drawers for folded items beneath). Less common in today's bedroom is the dressing-table, a common feature for centuries, which might contain hair brushes, scent, jewelry box and, most importantly, the mirror – a small reminder that the bedroom is the last private realm for our thoughts and selves.

left Worked in 1816 – the date is embroidered on one of the panels – this spectacular patchwork quilt is composed of a wonderful assortment of late-eighteenth- and early-nineteenth-century dress fabrics. It has pride of place in the best bedroom of this East London townhouse. Think of all the old scraps of material you have collected over the years, or old items of clothing that you no longer use – why not make use of them and create a personalized bed covering, throw or even curtains?

below, top An English fruitwood chair is draped with a nineteenth-century fine-wool tartan shawl.

below, bottom An early-nineteenth-century pony-skin trunk is packed with the owner's smartest tartan shawls for the long journey by sea and wagon to the New World.

opposite **William Morris** designed and produced some of the world's most sumptuous Arts and Crafts fabrics and wallpapers. Original Morris textiles, these late-nineteenth-century printed-linen bed hangings were discovered in a Scottish castle and brought triumphantly back to London. The curtains, although Victorian, illustrate the influence the Middle Ages had on Morris's work.

'Most part of it is furnished in the old style, as for example mama's and my apartment are brown wainscots, and the bed curtains and hangings are crimson damask laced with gold most dreadfully tarnished.'

Elizabeth Yorke upon visiting Wimpole Hall, Cambridgeshire, England in 1781

p. 95, clockwise, from top left An English table in the style of Sheraton (c. 1800) has oval handles cast with intertwining dolphins and holds a fine birch German Biedermeier travelling mirror and a pretty Coalport porcelain bowl, which is a useful receptacle for items of jewelry. A Federal oval toilet mirror sits atop an American chest of drawers in the master bedroom of a Manhattan apartment; candles cast a flattering light on the dresser's reflection and the wall behind, which is, in fact, a trompe l'oeil. This sturdy old oak Welsh cupboard opens to reveal the farmer's shirts within. An early-eighteenth-century oak table in a Shropshire manor house has just one piece resting on it – a striking tortoiseshell tea caddy, which makes a wonderful alternative jewelry box.

above left Everyone likes the luxury of a tall bed to swing their feet from; in an Irish country house, getting into that position is made a little more graceful by these ornate bed steps. The steps are covered to match the nineteenth-century chintz bed hangings. The magnificent display of textiles in this bedroom is a feast for the eyes. Also noteworthy is the cylindrical mahogany cupboard to the left of the bed, the purpose of which is to conveniently hide the chamber pots.

above right An early-nineteenth-century Irish bateau bed in the French Empire style. Luxurious red silk drapes swoop down from high above the bed, adding a touch of decadence to these otherwise unadorned sleeping quarters.

opposite An original length of woven Spitalfields silk hangs over the early-eighteenth-century marble fireplace and similar lengths of fine old textiles can create the same effect in any home, bringing a welcome softness to the bedroom. A patchwork quilt covers the bed, which has a late-nineteenth-century cast-iron framework with brass finials.

'The colours of the curtains and their fringe – the tints of crimson and gold – appear everywhere in profusion, and determine the *character* of the room.'

Edgar Allan Poe, *The Philosophy of Furniture*, 1840

left An Italian dressing room has a distinctly 1920s feel to it. Light filtered through the muslin curtains has softened the colours of the rose-patterned wall hanging over the years. Muslin is a fine fabric, making it a very agreeable material to have in the windows of the bedroom as it creates a light and floaty feeling. The dressing table and buttoned chair are positioned by the window to benefit from as much natural light as possible. Discretely feminine, this spacious room is almost two hundred years old.

opposite An excess of curtain fabric gathers at the foot of a cane chair in the bedroom of an Italian palazzo. It is easy to add a few extra centimetres to the length of a curtain and the effect is one of luxury and exuberance. The panels and both sides of the shutters in the bay window have been decorated to complement the paintwork on the door and surrounding walls. Hardly an inch of wall space has been left unadorned, although it is clear to see that some of the design has faded with the passing of years. We are left wondering just how tall this room is and whether the decoration continues on the ceiling.

opposite Heavy oak doors open to reveal neatly stacked linen, a yellow patchwork quilt and plaid shawls in a late-eighteenth-century sea-captain's house in London.

above left Most bedrooms contain a chair, which is used either as a reading or sewing seat or more likely as a place to lay out clothes. Here, a brass family crest is proudly displayed on a late-eighteenth-century English mahogany chair.

above right Painstakingly painted to simulate bamboo, this early-nineteenth-century beechwood chair rests lightly against seventeenth-century oak panelling in a Shropshire yeoman's house.

'When linen is well dried and laid by for use, nothing more is necessary than to secure it from damp and insects. It may be kept free of the latter by a judicious mixture of aromatic shrubs and flowers, cut up and sewed in silken bags, which must be interspersed among the drawers and shelves.'

Enquire Within Upon Everything, published by Houlston and Sons, 1887

Simple and cost-effective techniques can create wonderful effects, avoiding the need to purchase expensive materials. This Manhattan bedroom's walls are painted to simulate the marble of the 1860s mantelpiece and fireplace, which has an arched cast-iron register plate grate. From the hallway, with its turned balusters and mahogany handrail, you can see the bed covered in a reversible Victorian American wool quilt dating from 1848. Worn rugs are dotted around the room and ensure that sleepy risers do not step out of bed onto cold wooden floorboards.

opposite Large enough even for those with a vast collection of clothes, this wardrobe with its original white-lead paint, discoloured with time, is an unmissable addition to a bedroom. It is based on the proportions of a classical column: the section below the dado rail corresponds to the plinth, the main cupboard to the column itself and the frieze and cornice to the capital. In its lifetime, the wardrobe will probably have stored linen and items of clothing from embroidered waistcoats to crinolines to pencil skirts.

right The Oak Bedroom at Calke Abbey in Derbyshire has an elaborate nineteenth-century four-poster bed with barley-twist columns and attractive printed chintz. With a little effort, you can build a frame to transform your bed into a four-poster – it might not be an antique, but it will look as effective. This bed is surrounded by an accumulation of possessions – an old towel rail, cased natural-history specimens and a lacquered chest of drawers that are gilded and decorated with scenes from the Orient.

The principal bedroom in the Aitken-Rhett House in South Carolina has peeling emerald-green louvred shutters, which keep out the blistering midday sun while allowing gentle breezes to cool the room. Ideal for hot climates, shutters can be bought in DIY shops or salvage yards and are not hard to fix to the exterior wall, thereby avoiding the need for curtains. Evocative of a bygone age in the Deep South, this bedroom has wooden panelling up to dado height, intended to protect the wall from chairs and other furniture set against it. Matting covers most of the softwood floorboards, as is traditional in the tropics. Soft shades of green and orange add an air of serenity so necessary for inducing slumber in the stately bateau bed with its vivid mahogany veneer.

above Who could resist sinking onto this iron bedstead, heaped with cushions and bolsters covered in old French ticking, for a quick afternoon nap? The frame of this day bed is on castors and can be easily moved to follow the sun or to permit the recliner to stretch out in contemplation of the surrounding mountains of the Auvergne. It is easy to customize your own pillows and cushions by carefully selecting lengths of antique fabric.

'Lying late is not only hurtful by the relaxation it occasions, but also by occupying that part of the day at which exercise is so beneficial.'

Dr Wilson Philip, 'Treatise on Indigestion', 1887

left Against austere dark panelling and floorboards, the white and pink quilt looks soft and inviting in a farmhouse in Shropshire. Old handmade quilts can often be picked up in house sales and one such as this would probably have taken one person many months to make.

middle A hinged panel in an attic-bedroom door maintains a certain amount of privacy as morning tea or coffee can be left on the shelf attached to the exterior of the door without entering the room. The door, originally from a tailor's shop, still has red paint from the early-nineteenth century, which complements the tattered state of the upholstered baroque bed. This type of light switch, dating from the 1920s, has become so popular that copies are made nowadays.

right It is hard to tell whether this row of touchingly tiny girl's dresses belongs to the child whose East London bedroom this is, or whether they are used as an original form of wall decoration. The red and white striped quilt adds a boldness to the otherwise dainty setting.

pages 110–11 Snug and colourful, this Irish bedroom brings the sensation of sunny climes to the house. The bateau bed inlaid with walnut and satinwood dates from the late nineteenth century and is piled high with cushions. Faded tribal textiles, from the chair seats to the wall hangings, dominate the room, the only exception being the plain terracotta-painted blanket box by the bed. Despite the ethnic feel, the eighteenth-century country Chippendale chair fits comfortably into the room's composition. Even the bright oranges and yellows of the old Penguin books add to the cosy aura. As this room proves, you can introduce many patterns and decorated objects without jarring on the occupant's senses or destroying the room's unity.

above left Beautifully soft, well-worn kid gloves and silk bow ties are strewn carelessly on a gentleman's bedroom surface after a night on the town. A letter pokes out from a tooled leather correspondence box, maybe a note passed between admirers at the previous evening's event. Items such as these can easily be picked up in vintage stores or from antique dealers and add a historical elegance to the setting.

opposite Striking scarlet curtains billow out toward a smart tartan bedspread in a London townhouse. A much-used old elm clerk's desk dating from the 1790s is the perfect spot to sit and record your thoughts before retiring to bed, safe in the knowledge that others have been bent over that desk at the same occupation for centuries.

above right A leather travel toiletry box stores clothes brushes, flasks and has various compartments and sections. Missing patches of leather suggest that the case has been well used over the years, but its travelling days are probably now over.

left Deep-blue distempered walls set off the florid gilt mirror that reflects the four-poster bed in the sleeping quarters of a large house near Turin. Antique photo frames hold pictures of family members and sit on top of a painted wooden chest of drawers.

opposite A handsome four-poster bed in an Irish country house is reflected in a shabby gilt overmantel mirror whose glass is tarnished in places with spots of age. The sumptuous early-nineteenth-century gold-and-red bed hangings seem slightly frivolous with their tassels and baubles and are reminiscent of grand theatre curtains. It is worth looking out for theatre sales, where props are sold to the public. Mid-Victorian English Staffordshire figures and a dog stand on the mantelpiece. It is plain to see here that despite the differences in styles, the tradition of showing family photographs in the bedroom transcends national boundaries.

bathing

water ceremonies

What we expect as standard nowadays was as recently as 150 years ago a luxury. Modern plumbing and waste systems are taken for granted, yet barely fifty years ago many houses lacked these services. In fact, bathrooms in older houses are located

either in a modern extension or in a space that was never intended for this purpose. Perhaps because modern plumbing often suggests contemporary fittings, the characterful taps, tubs and lavatories that once bespoke a certain primitive quality today can be used in inventive and stylish ways. If we suspend the preoccupation with the all-white oasis of sterilized utilities, the bathroom can become a wholly different – and unexpected – confection of period details and quirky pieces.

ABOVE A simple wash bowl stands on the table in a French house near Clermont-Ferrand.
LEFT A tiny window in the bathroom of an East Berlin apartment has etched frosted glass and the frame has its original paint finish.
OPPOSITE A top-floor bathroom in a planter's house in South Carolina has luminous blue distempered walls. Water for the old hip bath is heated on the fire, which has a Greek revival chimney-piece.

At certain times in the past, at least in Western culture, bathing may have been viewed as a purely functional activity, but this has not always been the case. For those who could afford it, the aesthetics of the room, the fittings and the furniture, have held their own importance, something that is particularly relevant to us nowadays as we often focus on making bathing less of a necessity and more of a pleasure. It is here that we perform our daily rituals of hygiene and prepare ourselves for the outside world, but equally, it is in the bathroom that we unwind and pamper ourselves – truly a luxury of contemporary lifestyle.

Baths and showers themselves have changed very little since their invention, the most important advancement being that, generally speaking, they were not part of a central plumbing system until the late-nineteenth century. Before then, people cleaned themselves in moveable baths in the shape of a boot (upmarket versions of the tin bath) or in hip baths that were placed in bedrooms close to the fire and were filled by the jugful. Showers were used in grand eighteenth- and nineteenth-century houses, and some still survive, usually in houses that have seen little modernization in the last 150 years. Some even reflect the prevailing taste at the time and are painted to simulate bamboo.

By the second half of the nineteenth century, baths had evolved into the shape we recognize today. Initially, they were made of tin or zinc, but later cast-iron pieces with roll tops and decorative feet became popular. Feet are often the best indication of a bath's age, as the bath's basic shape has remained the same: feet from the Victorian period, for example, have claw and ball or florid rococo designs; by the early twentieth century, designs were often simpler cabriole shapes; and angular Art Deco designs were fashionable in the 1930s.

The predecessor to the modern wash-basin was the wash-stand, which usually comprised a marble top and an inset or freestanding bowl. Early-nineteenth-century examples (often without marble tops) were grained to resemble woods or decorated with such neoclassical imagery as urns, swags or classical figures. Later nineteenth-century examples had marble tops on stands of rich and exotic timbers carved in rococo and Italianate designs before Art Nouveau and Art Deco styles became fashionable. By the end of the nineteenth century, wash-stands fitted with taps were beginning to appear. As the twentieth century progressed, the concept of a bathroom suite with plumbed-in wash-basins gained popularity, signalling the end of wash-stands.

Modern-day bathroom styles seem to recommend uniformity in all elements – sink, tub, lavatory, bidet – and the bathroom 'suite' has become the norm. We must remember, however, that this is a twentieth-century phenomenon and not something that need be adhered to rigidly. Indeed, the bathroom is often neglected as a showcase for antique designs. We should see the difficulty of finding a matching unit as an advantage, an opportunity to select unusual fittings and elements to create a bathroom that is original and more personal.

The bathroom fitting with the least variation in design is the water closet, or lavatory. When one considers that many medieval houses had garderobes – small closets set within the thickness of the house's walls and which channelled the waste outside into the land or the moat – this won't seem a concession to modern needs. Garderobes were eventually replaced by chamber pots and closed stools, a moveable box on which you sat, much like a commode chair. The finest examples were upholstered in leather, baize or velvet, held in place with brass dome-headed tacks – materials all but lost in today's bathroom. In the second half of the nineteenth century, lavatories came into widespread use: seats were wooden (better ones in varnished hardwood, poorer ones in softwood). Grand residences had boxed and panelled mahogany versions, while some houses had delightful freestanding ceramic examples that were either multicoloured or decorated with flowers and birds. Lavatories became simpler affairs in the twentieth century, and were usually plain cream or white, although some Art Deco examples are green in colour.

Today it is possible to find late-nineteenth-century pieces, but the basic mechanics of the WC generally dictate using twentieth-century models. If you cannot find an old WC, the nineteenth-century boxed-and-panelled type is reasonably easy to re-create around a standard white lavatory.

Fittings can be bought as antiques from salvage yards or as reproductions. Occasionally, if lucky, you might come upon early tin fittings, such as a faux-bamboo shower. For that truly eighteenth-century feel, look out for the sculptural bath, placed freestanding in the bedroom.

'Until the house, until the room has been lived in, all looks inhuman, forbidding; it is only when the walls and their contents are redolent of human attention and human care, that the interior and its furniture can be a pride to its owner and a joy to those who see and use them.'

Halsey Ricardo, *The Modern Home*, 1909

Brass and lead were the two most essential materials for plumbing work right up until the mid-twentieth century. Lead was used for pipes, splashbacks and even to line the sinks themselves, whereas taps and bath plugs were more often made from brass. These taps may look like they were produced in the mid-nineteenth century, but they are in fact more recent garden taps going to show that certain designs remain ageless.

opposite Protected from prying eyes by old wooden Venetian blinds, this is a beautiful example of a French bathtub. Formed from zinc, the *Ménagère* was made in Paris in the late nineteenth century. Over a century of careful use has left the original deep-crimson paintwork intact. The marble effect with grey veining heightens the sense of luxury as the bather slips into the deep tub for a long soak. A touch of the new is seen in the floral display on the bath and in the fact that the bath's taps are plumbed in. This is a good example of how old and new can work side by side.

above left After numerous trips across the scrubbed floorboards with bucketfuls of hot water heated on the open fire, the relaxing waters are all the more enticing.

above right Used as a bathroom cabinet, this eighteenth-century cupboard is coated in American 'old barn red' paint.

'There is no part of the household arrangement so important as cheap convenience for personal ablution. For this purpose baths upon a large and expensive scale are by no means necessary; but though temporary or tin baths may be extremely useful upon pressing occasions, it will be found to be finally as cheap, and much more readily convenient, to have a permanent bath constructed.'

Enquire Within Upon Everything, published by Houlston and Sons, 1887

opposite You would be forgiven for thinking that this bathroom in an eighteenth-century château near Vichy had been tiled. It is in fact a clever illusion as the room is actually decorated with 1930s wallpaper, known as sanitary wallpaper, which has remained untouched since it was hung. A substantial cast-iron radiator warms the room. Radiators, such as this, can often be found in salvage yards; alternatively, reproductions are easy to come by.

below The stylish Art Deco inspired wash-basin and bidet are fed by old lead pipes. In spite of its age, the simple white porcelain brings a contemporary feel to the room.

left Wanting to integrate old fittings into the plumbing of a modern bathroom need not be a difficult task. In an eighteenth-century house in London, an enamelled cast-iron roll-top bath stands on bare floorboards, and a wash-stand and bowl have been connected to the taps and pipes of the bathroom. These old fittings sit happily with more modern items like the stainless-steel mirror.

opposite This fine eighteenth-century cast-iron hob grate keeps the bather warm on leaving the bath and heats up his outfit for the day. Fireplaces have often been boarded up over the centuries – this means that when uncovered, you will often find stunning fire surrounds and grates that have been protected for years. Wood has been treated in many different ways in this room; painted, polished, varnished and scrubbed surfaces come together to form a snug environment.

above This exotic bathroom in a former slave house in South Carolina is dominated by a bust of a Greek god and an American nineteenth-century cheval mirror. Reproduction busts can be bought, but it is sometimes more fun to search out the worn and chipped busts that appear in car boot sales or in antique shops. The verdant natural surroundings seen through the windows intensify the sultry southern feel.

left A completely unique look has been created in this commodious London bathroom, one that draws on styles from around the world to produce a universal appeal. Faded oriental rugs lie over the wooden floorboards and the walls are covered with Victorian picture frames. Some of these 'Oxford' frames (recognized by their crossed corners) contain large three-dimensional funeral cards, which are embossed with images of sarcophagi, gothic tracery, weeping willows and bowed figures to signify death and the world beyond. Chipped and scratched dark-wood panelling contrasts beautifully with the wall painted in a refreshing yellow and the fresh pinks of the large shell. A nineteenth-century cast-iron bath, a boldly angled sink and a lavatory with a high-level cistern with ornate brackets, make up the practical elements of the bathroom.

opposite A white bathroom always looks appealing and this one is made slightly more so by the pretty white petticoats hung to dry over the 1930s heated brass towel rail and by the contrasting dark wood of the door, floor and table. Floor-to-ceiling curtains in a soft pink chintz make the room feel older and more luxurious than a modern-day blind would.

below left Looking down into this compact bathroom, the eye is drawn to a modern version of a boxed-in lavatory.

Walnut panels cover all sides of the lavatory bowl, while a hole cut out of the top panel forms the seat. This style of WC was first introduced in the eighteenth century. Seashells have been a common bathroom ornament for many centuries.

below right An Edwardian nightshirt, probably purchased from an antiques' dealer specializing in fabric, has been hung up next to a German Biedermeier mirror in a London bathroom, while its owner takes a hot bath.

outdoor rooms

re-imagining the indoor–outdoor space

The design to bring the garden indoors and to extend the house outside is not a new concept. Plants have been brought inside for centuries, whether on a grand scale, tulips displayed in extravagant tiered Delft vases; or on a simpler level, plants were  often placed on the windowsills of cottages to brighten up the vista. Bringing plants inside for decoration or for their protection has helped to create rooms that naturally link the house and garden, halfway houses where plants come in and furniture goes out, where our interest in nature and horticulture is encouraged, but can be enjoyed from the weather-free comfort of the outdoor room.

ABOVE Rows of terracotta pots in storage. LEFT This cast-bronze decoration on a New York roof terrace was rescued from the ruins of a late-nineteenth-century warehouse in Lower Manhattan. OPPOSITE A charming outdoor potting shed in Spitalfields, London.

PAGES 134–35, LEFT TO RIGHT The gardener's bothy at Calke Abbey, Derbyshire has old seed drawers and intense-blue limewashed walls on which a row of hooks and an old clock have been hung. Old cupboards in an outdoor room in Derbyshire store garden implements and are plastered with prize certificates from a local horticultural show.

For hundreds of years, those who could afford them have built spaces for the maximum enjoyment and appreciation of nature. Such rooms have developed according to local climates and horticulture, not to mention setting. Some spaces, which are typically connected to the main residence, are called the garden room and are used for entertainment and relaxation with conventional features like windows and fireplaces. Separate structures, such as a summerhouse or gazebo, might resemble a Greek temple or a gothic turret, functioning as a decorative object in a larger landscape. Each indoor-outdoor space has its own allure as the scents of the garden waft in and we feel at one with either our mastery or our awe of nature.

No building illustrates our desire to commune with nature and plants better than the greenhouse. Originally used as a place to propagate and protect fragile plants, such as citrus trees, greenhouses have been incorporated into the grounds of large country houses and villas since the seventeenth century. Aptly named orangeries, they also provided an exotic refuge from the main house. Such buildings were usually built of stone or brick with conventional windows. Later, the concept of a glasshouse, where potted plants were kept on stages, gained popularity. Stone construction gave way to timber and glass, and by the time J. C. Loudon patented the curved cast-iron glazing bar for use in greenhouses in 1816, conservatories could be found attached to countless smaller country houses.

Nineteenth-century technology brought new forms of conservatory construction. Built from iron or timber or a mixture of both, these outdoor rooms took on a variety of forms and degrees of ornamentation; gothic and Italianate were particularly popular. Some were full-blown conservatories, others simple glazed porches, lean-tos or glazed corridors across a courtyard. Windows were sometimes filled with coloured glass, and floors covered in decorative tiles. Urns, cast-iron seats, statuary and other embellishments filled their interiors. After World War I, the popularity of such manifestly delicate structures as a living space waned, although greenhouses for horticulture survived. It is only in recent years, perhaps catalyzed by new concerns about our environment and a renewed love of nature, that the conservatory has become popular again. Nowadays a large number of companies supply off-the-peg and bespoke conservatories.

Other, less impressive garden structures are fun to use and adapt. Outhouses, potting sheds, bothies, washhouses and old earth closets often survive the tidying influence of modern living. Frequently unused and overlooked, they may well have become the dumping ground for obsolete furniture, plant pots or tools. They will also have been subject to the effects of fluctuating humidity levels, which will have given them a very particular unconscious beauty in their weathered wood and shabby paintwork.

Just as important as the structure that encourages our interaction with the outdoors is its contents. Historic interiors and buildings have taught us that objects, whether of utility or of decoration, can animate the outdoor room and reinforce our relationship with nature. Galvanized watering cans, folding iron tables, slatted café chairs and old terracotta plant pots – all are practical objects that are as happy inside as out, that recall past activities and link our human activities to nature. It is important to remember that practical and recreational purposes can be easily combined in outdoor rooms. Plant propagation and tending and the storage of garden materials are activities that happily share space with such pastimes as reading, writing, eating and drinking.

Outdoor rooms have experienced the ravages of time to a greater degree than a house's interior, as is illustrated in this gardener's retreat in Derbyshire where the blue limewash has in places come away from the wall to reveal the brickwork underneath. Never neglect to look at what treasures old outhouses have on your land. The space contains miscellaneous items of gardening equipment and a fire offers some comfort to the pottering gardener on cold winter days.

pages 138–39 This gardener's bothy in central England has been filled with hundreds of terracotta plant pots brought in for the winter from a vast walled garden. Higgledy-piggledy shelving at the back of the room holds saws and brackets and the worn bench next to it is where the gardener is carrying out his winter repairs. A dedicated gardener has labelled the old seed drawers and an ancient glass cloche by the window is used to protect delicate seedlings. The room has been laid out so that everything is to hand.

left It was only after the end of World War II that this sandstone outside convenience, with its small rectangular window that allows natural light into the otherwise unlit space, ceased to be used for its original purpose, instead becoming more of a garden shed. This would be the perfect place to germinate seeds or to store items away from direct sunlight. In the grounds of a château outside Clermont-Ferrand, France, an uneven cobbled pathway leads up to the tired ochre-coloured door whose bottom corner has disintegrated over the years and lost its paint.

opposite The cupboards and walls of an old outbuilding have been blackened by the soot of the room's fireplace, and a half-door with casement window above affords a good view of the back stairs and entrance to the Aitken-Rhett house in Charleston, South Carolina.

opposite Extending the living space outdoors, an informal seating area is situated in a corner of an eighteenth-century London townhouse. Two simple iron chairs sit on a carpet of gravel, while the bowed iron table stands on a cracked stone slab. Years of damp conditions have turned the garden furniture into colours that complement the natural setting. A tranquil haven in which to relax with a glass of wine at the end of the day.

above, left to right Intended for outdoor use, this 1920s café chair is an excellent choice of garden furniture and is still decorated in its original red paint. The number on the chair back indicates which establishment it belongs to. A galvanized watertank has been taken from its natural home in the attic and now holds goldfish in the garden. We consider the layout of the outdoor room in essentially the same way as that of an interior space. Here, nineteenth-century terracotta pots line a London garden's sandstone steps that link the indoor–outdoor spaces.

'Where there is a garden of tolerable extent, some of the principal apartments, supposing the situation proper, may be very conveniently placed in the hinder part of the house. They will by these means be freed from noise and disturbance, and will have good light; the garden will also be a good prospect.'

Isaac Ware, *The Complete Body of Architecture*, 1756

above, left to right Outdoor living is enlivened with a bold use of colour even if it has seen much wear and tear: an outhouse at Calke Abbey, Derbyshire has peeling ochre limewash and an oxidized brass door knob; an early-eighteenth-century carved stone head holds a bronze water spout in the grounds of a château in southern France; and exotic russet limewash has been used on the walls of a north Italian castello.

opposite At first glance, this French tackle room looks as if it is completely lined with wood; in fact, the walls are limewashed and much of the wood panelling has been removed over the years leaving only a few old shelves and tackle pegs. If you are lucky enough to have an outbuilding on your land, they can be easily adapted to suit your purposes, but do try not to destroy the charm of their patina.

pages 146–47 Built partly into the hillside, this outdoor scullery would never have been dry, so the walls were covered in 'dolly-blue' limewash and stone was used for the floor. Heavily scrubbed pine and sycamore shelves, plate rack and drawers and a row of sturdy old sinks with brass taps add to the pleasing decay to create a very evocative interior.

The conservatory is the most popular outdoor room. This space combines the comfort of the inside with the light and feel of the outside, enhancing the indoor–outdoor relationship primarily through its use of glass. Joining an eighteenth-century silkweaver's house in London with its garden, this conservatory is used mainly as a reading room and has deep upholstered Victorian chairs with faded and torn chintz covers. There is also a work bench where plants are potted and the orchids are tended. Avid nurturers of orchids, the owners display some of their prize specimens in old terracotta pots on the shelves behind the armchairs. Care has been taken to bond the zone's indoor and outdoor elements in the choice of colours – the flowers' natural shades of pink complement the hues in the floral textiles of the chairs. Electric lighting introduces today's technology to the space so that it can also be used in the evening.

'The brilliancy of the lighting; the graceful arrangement and lavish profusion of the flowers, the soft shade and the delicate twilight of the beautiful conservatory; together with the elegant and fanciful decorations bestowed on the canopied elevation prepared, very nearly in the form of a throne, for the Regent, produced an effect that was altogether dazzling.'
Frances Trollope, *The Days of the Regency*, 1848

'Eclecticism is our fate; we take what we find, this for its beauty, that for its convenience, and that for its antiquity, and another thing even for its ugliness; thus we live amid flotsam, as if the end of the world were near.'

Alfred de Musset, *La confession d'un enfant du siècle*, 1836

left The corner of this conservatory is dedicated to garden chores, with two recently planted bulbs still on the potting bench. A wicker basket is a good storage solution that fits unobtrusively into its surroundings. This room suggests that on a thorough rummage around, many treasures would be unearthed, such as long-forgotten household items and antique garden tools.
right A novel use for an architect's old plan chest, which now stores garden equipment; the narrow drawers are ideal for seeds, bulbs and such implements as secateurs and trowels. On top of the wooden unit are two packing cases, from the renowned London department store Liberty and the Whitbread brewery.

An old warehouse in the garden plot of an East London house has been converted into a wonderful top-lit space that can be used for relaxing on lazy Sunday afternoons, but is also the perfect spot for parties. The interior is minimalist in style, but nonetheless has unique antique items; for example, the patterned iron grating, unusual three-legged table and the dressmaker's mannequin. A potting bench against the wall shows that the more traditional activities associated with garden buildings also take place here. The space is a charming medley of scrubbed, faded and worn pine boarding and flooring.

details and techniques

• hallways • staircases • panelling • flooring

• fireplaces • storage • collecting • displaying

• decorative plaster • textiles • wallpaper

• painted furniture • wall finishes • gilding

• flat oil paint • limewash • graining

The entrance be it a pillared marble hall in a grand house or a simple lobby in a humble cottage is in effect a public space. As a reception area, its decoration is often in a more formal architectural style than the inner rooms; it is here that guests have their first impressions of a place and are offered a taste of what's to come.

When space and financial constraints do not permit the use of such materials as stone or marble, walls can be painted to simulate large masonry blocks or carved stone (see opposite) and timber pilasters can be disguised to appear like more costly materials. The eighteenth and nineteenth centuries saw furniture designed specifically for the entrance hall: hall chairs with solid backs often in the shape of a shield and which in the grandest homes were decorated with a family crest; arched and upholstered leather porters' chairs protected footmen from draughts; marble-topped tables (see below left) held salvers for visiting cards and a post box for letters; and trophies in the form of animal heads from hunts around the world hung on the walls. More modest homes can also create a striking look: pine can be grained to resemble oak panelling, while dados and cornices give classical form to relatively small spaces.

hallways

staircases

Not only a means of connecting one floor to another, a staircase is a marker of the social status of a house and frequently an expression of the builder's creativity. Like fireplaces they are influenced by the whims of fashion, although their size and degree of decoration is also dependent upon their position within a house, for example, whether they are the principal (see top) or secondary, 'back' staircase (see bottom). Their very construction and use means they are especially vulnerable to wear and tear (see opposite, top right).

Staircases were restricted to larger houses in medieval times, but in the sixteenth century, the open-well staircase was developed – a series of flights rising around an open square or rectangle (see opposite, bottom middle). Wooden handrails were supported on balusters that sit on either a closed string,

i.e. a continuous rail sloping up the staircase (see middle), or an open string, i.e. the step itself (see opposite, bottom right). Stone steps with iron balustrades were particularly popular in Italy and France (see opposite, bottom left).

In the seventeenth century, classical design gained influence and softwood began to replace local materials – balusters were turned in urn shapes with simple doric columns (see opposite, top left) and sometimes set in pairs or threes on the step of the staircase itself (see opposite, top second from left).

Late-eighteenth- and early-nineteenth-century federal, and regency staircases generally had simple square balusters (see bottom). As the nineteenth-century progressed, fashionable staircases acquired heavier detailing: turned balusters and prominent newels rising above the handrail (see top).

panelling

Timber has been used to line the interiors of houses since the late Middle Ages, reaching a peak in quality and design in the sixteenth and seventeenth centuries. Sixteenth-century 'wainscotting', as it was known, is either characterized by small panels with heavily moulded surrounds or carving simulating cloth ('linenfold panelling'). Joints are pegged and the panelling is sometimes painted with symmetrical designs, text or at the end of the century Renaissance motifs. In humbler houses and attic spaces simple muntin and plank – jointed vertical studs and planks – is a popular type of timber partition, attached to a beam at the top and a rail at the base.

Deal and other softwoods from the Baltic revolutionized panelling and its design at the end of the seventeenth century, making the creation of larger panels possible and the jointing of the timber easier. Wall panelling corresponded to the classical order in that the skirting represented the base, the dado or chair rail the pedestal, the wall space the column and the cornice the entablature. The colour of panelling generally reflects the use of the rooms: dark oak or dark painted for dining rooms and entrance halls; lighter finishes, frequently painted pine, for drawing rooms.

Painted tongue-and-groove boarding is suitable for such utilitarian areas as kitchens, sculleries, pantries and bathrooms, and can also be used to line old ceilings especially when in poor repair. Lincrusta, a thick moulded wallpaper, provides a cheap alternative to panelling, especially below dado rails in halls and some designs even simulate oak panelling, a fashion that was particularly popular during the 1920s and 1930s.

flooring

Nothing affects the atmosphere of a room more than the treatment of the floor, yet its covering is frequently the last part of the room we think about and until recently the fashion has been to cover it completely with fitted carpet. Luckily, with old houses come old floors, often in poor condition and needing careful repair, but timber, stone, brick and tile surfaces can all look wonderful if treated properly.

Although the earliest floors were of beaten earth, timber has been used since Roman times. Clues to the date of a building can be found in the components that make up the structure of a timber floor because joists and beams have changed over the centuries in their material, section, size and decoration. The best quality floorboards are composed of hardwood and until the early-nineteenth-century, when steam-powered mechanical saws cut boards to identical dimensions, board widths were not standardized. Boards generally became narrower as time progressed, influenced by cost issues and the growing popularity of fitted carpets laid over boards never intended to be seen.

When repairing or patching wooden floors, it is important to work with the same timber and to retain as much old material as possible. We are now used to seeing boards varnished or polished, but many years ago pine floors had a dry whitish appearance achieved by 'dry scrubbing'. Today you can bleach pine boards with a lime putty – beware this is a dangerous material and requires goggles and plastic gloves – which is left on the surface for thirty minutes and then removed. When dry, the boards should be waxed with a clear or white floor wax.

Stone was used for flooring in well-to-do households or in areas where it was quarried locally; with time it became the common floor covering for kitchens, halls and cellars. Squares of light-coloured stone or marble were frequently alternated with squares of such darker materials as slate. In places where quarried stone was unavailable but clay deposits existed, brick or quarry-tile (known by various names including pammets, see below second from right) floors were common. France and Italy are particularly noted for their terrazzo and tiled floors (see opposite, second from left and below left).

fireplaces

The fireplace is regarded as the heart of the room and is often the space's strongest visual element. Designs have developed over the centuries as fashion has dictated and technology has improved. Nowadays we think of fireplaces as set into either a chimney breast or the wall, and although they existed in this way in medieval times, they were confined to the grandest buildings. Most of our forebears cooked on open fires in the centre of the room. Later, open fires were contained within smoke bays or under smoke hoods – partitions of wattle and daub, lath and plaster, stone or brick, which funnelled the smoke up through the roof. At the end of the sixteenth century, however, chimney stacks and wall (mural) fireplaces became the norm.

Even by the end of the seventeenth century only wealthy homes had more than one fireplace. Grander houses had fireplaces with chamfered or moulded jambs and lintels and four-centred arches made from stone, brick or timber. The mantelpieces above were usually made from carved plaster, wood or timber panelling, but new designs were introduced at the end of the seventeenth century. At first these were simple moulded surrounds without shelves and constructed in wood, marble or stone (see middle), but they soon evolved into flat panelled jambs and lintels in simple baroque shapes, sometimes with a carved console as a keystone.

By the eighteenth century the fireplace had acquired more than a practical role. Just as the altar was the centrepiece in a Greek or Roman temple, the mantelpiece was the focal point of a polite room. Indeed, architects chose classical imagery and motifs to decorate their fireplaces, and in Roman Catholic countries this area was sometimes used as a shrine and held a religious image flanked by candles. Neoclassicism was the best-known style of the period, notably interpreted by Scottish architect Robert Adam to produce light elegant effects through classical decoration in relief (see opposite, middle).

Behoving its position as a statement of taste, expensive marble was used on the best fireplaces. In middle-class homes, marble was at first reserved for the fireplace slips (see opposite, middle and right); however, by the early-nineteenth century full marble surrounds were affordable to a wider population. As the nineteenth century progressed, designs became more eclectic and a wider variety of materials were used, such as slate and cast-iron. At the end of the nineteenth century a note of order did appear in the design of the domestic interior: Art Nouveau in France, Jugendstil in Germany and the Arts and Crafts Movement favoured fireplace designs that were fully integrated with the room's décor and furniture.

Modern living requirements and new techniques of heating have resulted in fireplaces being blocked, their mantelpieces removed and their place as the focus of the room replaced by the television set. Simply opening up a neglected fireplace gives new lifeblood to a room and reintroduces a practical source of heat.

165 details and techniques

You may not think it, but old houses often have cupboards that are fitted into the fabric of the building and are intended for specific uses, dependent upon where they are situated and how they are designed.

Until the seventeenth century, clothes were hung on wooden hooks or folded and placed in a chest. However, the development of the wardrobe and the chest of drawers meant that clothing could be protected from dust and linen could be neatly folded and placed in drawers or on shelves. By the nineteenth century, some city houses had walk-in linen closets and fitted wardrobes, which often flanked the chimney breast in a bedroom.

Food was stored either in pantries or in a cupboard by the main fireplace if a dry space was needed. Large seventeenth-century open fireplaces frequently contained recesses in which spices and salt were kept dry; this so-called 'spice cupboard' often had wooden doors to keep out soot. Freestanding and sometimes fitted oak court cupboards made between the mid-seventeenth and mid-eighteenth centuries would house both food and china. As kitchen ranges replaced open hearths, so fitted cupboards flanking the chimney breast became more popular. This arrangement remained the accepted storage place for dry food and china until well into the twentieth century and is found in thousands of back living areas or kitchens in terraced houses in the UK and the USA.

Fitted cupboards are frequently a wonderful archaeological tool; not only do they often still have old fittings and pegs, but many have also retained their original decorative schemes within. Ignored for generations and unaffected by the ravages of light, vivid colours and striking patterns on old paint surfaces and wallpaper provide exciting glimpses of the past.

storage

collecting

That most idiosyncratic of rooms, the museum is somewhere to house and display artefacts collected on travels. By the eighteenth century the craze for collecting meant that many houses had museum rooms, or sometimes simply a small cabinet of curiosities in the living area devoted to the unusual and the exotic.

In some houses the families were so excited by these objects that they became part of the decoration of principal rooms, as in this stuffed bear in an Irish house (opposite, above right). At Calke Abbey in Derbyshire, for example, much of the house was given over to the Harpur-Crewe's passion for collecting natural history.

Entrance halls, corridors and lobbies are lined with glass cases full of geological specimens, birds' eggs and shells, and even the grandest room in the house – the Saloon – is dominated by the family's extraordinary collection of taxidermy. Whatever you collect, make a statement and create a unique form of room decoration.

displaying

As the ruins of ancient Greece and Rome were studied and unearthed, the interest in classical design, sculpture and the antique became a passion for architects and the wealthy amateur alike. In the eighteenth century a trip to see the original ruins of ancient Greece and Rome, The Grand Tour, became an important part of the education of the young gentleman. Those who could afford to buy original sculpture did so (see top left and bottom left) and brought them back home; the less wealthy had to content themselves with plaster casts (see top middle and bottom right). Often both would be mixed in a collection as copies of the most famous pieces were seen as essential. Famous contemporary figures and members of the family were often sculpted in the guise of Roman gods, caesars and senators. Special podiums and carved brackets (see middle right) were created to support the sculpture.

As with all fashion, this rage filtered down to the middle classes, with plaster casts adorning the libraries and studies of more modest homes. To meet this demand, the nineteenth century saw great museums make replicas of famous pieces both for sale and to fill their own galleries, eliminating the need to travel abroad to study these marvels. Such was the growing interest in archaeology.

decorative plaster

The gentle lines of old plasterwork on ceilings and walls add much to the softness and charm of a house's interior. By carrying out patch repairs rather than wholesale replastering, one can avoid creating a room that is sterile and lifeless. Plasterwork is one of the first places to show structural stress and strain; its fragile nature means that it is easily damaged by water, knocks and structural movement, so cracks, bulges and crumbling plaster are often found. This does not indicate, however, that it should be stripped and replastered, rather lovingly restored.

Lime was used traditionally for internal plasterwork, and was applied in three coats. The two rough undercoats were mixed with cow, goat or horse hair as a binder and finished with a smoother top coat. Where plaster was not being applied to a masonry wall, i.e. on a partition or ceiling, a backing material was necessary. In the Middle Ages, this would have been woven wattle (usually hazel twigs); riven timber laths were in use by the seventeenth century – made of pine, beech or oak – and remained the most-used

backing until the middle of the twentieth century and the advent of plasterboard.

By the late eighteenth century, plaster composed of gypsum or plaster of Paris was used primarily for decorative plaster ornament and was cast in hardwood moulds of boxwood, wax or gelatine; nowadays rubber moulds are used. Fibrous plaster, patented in 1856, had a dramatic effect upon plasterwork. Hitherto most decorative plaster-work had been worked in situ; now, large sections of decorative plasterwork reinforced with canvas could be manufactured in workshops and then transported to site later.

Elaborately moulded and decorated ceilings were common in wealthy houses in the sixteenth- and seventeenth centuries: heavy cornices, mouldings forming panels, hanging pendants and cast or freehand ornament. In the eighteenth century, these became even more elaborate with rococo, neoclassical and gothic designs across the ceiling. The early-nineteenth century saw a change in direction, with much simpler ceilings, influenced by the Greek revival movement and more sober classicism.

All too often plaster mouldings and cornices were removed as they were erroneously regarded as unimportant. If your home has no remaining mouldings, investigate houses of the same date in the neighbourhood. It is also important to consider the status of a room, taking care not to insert over-elaborate designs. Replacing missing cornices can be undertaken by either creating the cornice in situ, or by casting and then fixing the ornament in place. To undertake the former, a competent plasterer is needed. Casting involves using original lengths of cornice as a template to make a mould. This mould is produced by making a rubber or clay squeeze of existing details, then casting in plaster of Paris. Again, a job for the professional.

Remember when patching old plaster, check what material was used and patch like with like, for example, lime with lime. Original decoration is best salvaged and refitted into replacement sections of plasterwork. Off the peg mouldings are generally rather crude, although certain companies now supply authentic designs.

textiles

The appeal of old textiles lies partly in their fragility. More susceptible to the effects of light and time than such robust materials as stone or wood, textiles are quick to show disintegration and wear. By their very nature, they are a tangible and often deeply personal link to people who have used them over the years.

Textiles are all around us: we clothe ourselves in them, furniture is upholstered in them, they cover our beds and we walk on them. Their history stretches back to the origins of human existence. A number of types of textiles have survived some hundreds of years and can still be enjoyed although they are vulnerable to wear, insect damage and light. It is essential, therefore,

that we are vigilant in our care and use of them, so we can hand them down to future generations.

The beauty of the late-nineteenth-century Knole sofa covered in its original red velvet (opposite, below, third from left) lies ultimately in its textile sheath that is now so delicate its owners do not sit upon it, using it instead as a piece of sculpture well away from natural daylight. The patchwork quilt dated 1816 (above right) has been passed down the family and is made of rare dress fabrics from the late-eighteenth- and early-nineteenth centuries, a wonderful link to the everyday life of the maker. Good use has been made of the William Morris window curtains (c. 1880), now hanging around a four-poster (below left); furthermore, they are kept away from direct sunlight.

Whether we inherit or scour antique shops for textiles that give our homes a gentle time-worn appearance, we do need to stop and consider for a while how we are going to use them without destroying their intrinsic history and their beauty – that very special pleasing decay.

wallpaper

Rarely is one lucky enough to inherit old wallpaper in good condition with a house. More usual is to find fragments of wallpaper hidden behind architraves, skirting, panelling or within cupboards.

Wallpaper probably originated in China and was certainly in use in Europe by the sixteenth century. By the eighteenth century it was quite commonly used worldwide in wealthy and middle-class homes, and was manufactured in a number of places, notably England and France. Initially designs were hand-painted, stencilled or printed with wood blocks; later designs were printed with metal blocks and by the 1760s cylinder printing was in use. However, it was not until the early-nineteenth century that mechanized cylinders came into their own, leading to the mass production of wallpaper in many colours on continuous lengths of paper. By the mid-eighteenth century, oil was employed to create colouring, gradually replacing the earlier water-based and distemper colours and achieving greater colour intensity and accuracy in printing.

As with all interior decoration, wallpaper designs have been greatly influenced by changing fashions and technology. For instance, hand-painted Chinese papers decorated with birds, flowers and landscapes were in demand throughout the eighteenth century; in the second half of the eighteenth century neoclassical and gothic designs became popular; and the manufacture of flock wallpaper – powdered wool stuck to paper – provided a new type of wall covering in France and England (see opposite, top middle). France was renowned for its printed papers depicting classical scenes (see bottom middle), which were particularly popular in the early-nineteenth century. Sanitary wallpaper, which usually imitated brickwork or tiling (see opposite, top right), was produced in large quantities in the 1930s to line the walls of bathrooms.

Removal of old paper is best left to a professional conservator, who can also advise on original colouring and dating. A number of companies produce reproductions of old wallpapers and certain companies will undertake the costly business of reproducing specific designs.

painted furniture

Most old painted furniture is usually either from the below stairs areas of a house or from the summerhouse and garden pavilion, the reason for which was to hide or disguise inferior woods. Nonetheless, it does have a long history of use in the smart parts of a house throughout the world. Scandinavia has its folk furniture decorated with texts, figures and flowers, while its sophisticated Gustavian furniture was in simple greys and whites. France and Italy are well-known for their painted and gilded furniture and England for its early-nineteenth-century faux bamboo chairs and bedroom suites (opposite, bottom left).

Kitchen cupboards and tables were frequently painted, in both large and small houses (opposite, top left and right), with only worktops left bare. It is, however, to the interiors of cupboards that we often need to turn to see strong colours – eighteenth-century corner cupboards had intense peacock blues (opposite, top second from right) and rich reds.

Above stairs at Calke Abbey, the charming late-eighteenth-century gothic ladderback (opposite, top second from left) was intended for a garden pavilion. Portraits from the period often show painted garden furniture.

Unfortunately, with the fashion for stripped pine in recent years, many beautiful and rare paint finishes have been removed from furniture. Yet much survives and can be cherished for the future and, of course, furniture can be repainted in the original style (see flat oil paint p. 184).

wall finishes

Highly decorative schemes other than wallpaper, painting or stencilling have been employed in the homes of the wealthy for centuries. Some of the grandest houses of the seventeenth- and eighteenth centuries had great murals painted by Italian and French painters such as Antonio Verrio and Louis Laguerre, who together with native artists brought this technique to northern Europe, decorating the great baroque halls and staircases of the wealthy. Walls were often painted with allegorical and historical scenes between classical columns (see above middle), while the ceiling above was represented as the sky with gods and goddesses rising or resting among the clouds. This tradition of wall painting survived in certain countries, especially Italy and France, well into the twentieth century.

An extremely sophisticated and complex painted wall decoration, trompe l'oeil gives a convincing three-dimensional illusion of reality. Illustrated here are examples from northern Italy (see above left and opposite, middle) and New York (see opposite, left), all in a classical vein with busts and other Greek and Roman imagery.

The New York room has been decorated to appear as a grotto with rusticated stonework in the ruins of ancient Rome.

Print rooms employ another form of wall decoration. These reached a zenith of popularity in the latter half of the eighteenth- and early-nineteenth centuries. Engravings of portraits, classical scenes, caricatures of famous and political figures or the comedy of human existence were pasted onto walls already lined with paper. These were framed by printed borders pasted on afterwards and were sometimes coloured in with watercolours to produce a colourful effect. This was often a pastime of the wealthy, who would spend hours arranging the images to produce the desired look. At Castletown House near Dublin (see top right), the print room was probably created by Lady Louisa Conolly and her sister in the late-eighteenth-century. The Irish Georgian Society produces printed sheets of borders for those wishing to create their own print room or cover a screen. Photocopies of old engravings onto good quality paper is a way of reducing the cost and avoiding damaging now valuable original prints by pasting them onto walls.

gilding

I, CÆSAR

Gilding timber or plaster has always been the activity of the affluent. Picture and mirror frames and consoles for statuary are typical examples, while in the homes of the very rich whole pieces of furniture were gilded. Panelling has been gilded since medieval times and eighteenth-century interiors often had gilt fillets (decorative carved or cast borders) fitted around wallpaper or silk hangings.

A variety of materials can be gilded from timber and metal to plaster and cast composite ornament. There are, however, only two methods of gilding: water gilding and oil gilding. Both use gold leaf in single squares, either loose or attached to tissue transfers. As their names suggest, water gilding is applied with water and oil gilding with an oil size. Although gilding can be put directly on the surface of an object, usually two intermediate layers are used. The first, gesso, is a coat of plaster painted onto the object to build up a layer of 1 to 4mm. On top of this a coloured layer of paint, called bole, is added, which comes in a number of different hues, most commonly red and ochre.

Water gilding is an immediate process, examples of which appear in the picture and mirror frames opposite (left column). Water and a small amount of rabbit glue are painted on top of the bole and the gold leaf is immediately applied with a flat brush. The gold adheres to the bole and should be left to dry until the gesso layer sounds slightly hollow when tapped. At this point, the surface is burnished by a smooth piece of jade, polishing the gold surface to such a degree that it appears metallic. Traditionally, only certain parts of the surface were burnished to provide highlights.

Oil gilding (as seen on the support for a bust opposite, bottom right), is a more simple technique. In place of the water and glue on top of the bole, oil size is painted on and allowed to dry until it is tacky. The time this takes varies according to the type of size used – some take three hours, some less. The gold is then applied with a flat brush and the whole allowed to dry. Oil gilding cannot be burnished and tends, therefore, to have a flatter less metallic look, which is often yellower in colour.

flat oil paint

Before the introduction of modern oil paints, timberwork was usually finished with lead-based paints. Often glossy when first applied, these went matt within two or three years, and it is this finish we usually find on old painted surfaces. Not only are the colours soft, but dry, two-tone and chalky, giving a wonderful feeling of depth. The colour palette was restricted, partly by the availability of pigments, and partly by the cost of manufacture. Readily obtainable and cheap earth pigments were therefore most common – brown, red, ochre, umber and grey. More exotic colours such as peacock blue and smalt (potash silicate strongly coloured with cobalt oxide and reduced to a powder) were introduced as paint technology advanced in the eighteenth and nineteenth centuries.

Apart from the obvious aesthetic advantages, lead paint generally has better adhesion than modern oil paints i.e. it sticks to the surface longer, in due course crumbling rather than peeling off. Lead paint can be harmful, and health and safety regulations have had the effect of marginalizing its use and it has been banned in some countries. With this in mind, where new paint is required, flat oil will produce the nearest effect, which can be made more realistic by diluting the paint slightly with white spirit and applying thinner coats. Special care is advised when dealing with old lead paint and particular caution is urged when sanding or scraping off the old paint. Suppliers of flat oil paint can be found on p. 191.

limewash

The walls of farmhouses, cottages and below stairs in grander houses were traditionally painted with limewash. Characterized by subtle variations in tone and texture due to the natural earth pigments and binders used in its manufacture, limewash weathers and ages in a particularly delicate and graceful way unlike modern wall paints.

Composed of lime putty and water it can be applied without pigments, known as whitewash, which when wet is translucent and when dry and in sunny conditions becomes an intense white. Coloured limewash, however, was widely used and pigments were obtained from various sources. For example, red ruddle or raddle, a soft red ironstone commonly used to mark sheep, produced a bright pink when mixed with limewash (see opposite left). Pinks and reds are created by mixing such fruit as crushed blackberries or damsons, or even by adding animals' blood.

The below stairs and service areas at Calke Abbey in Derbyshire, UK (owned by the British National Trust) and the Aitken-Rhett House in Charleston, South Carolina, USA (owned by the Historic Charleston Foundation) are painted with various traditional limewash colours, most striking of which is probably the 'dolly blue', so-called because the blue pigment was used in the bags manufactured by Reckitts and Colman to give your washing a 'blue white'. Particularly popular in kitchens, pantries and outside earth closets because its colour was thought to repel flies, it can be seen in its full vividness here (see opposite right and above right). One of the great advantages of limewash is its porosity. As with other lime-based materials it allows walls to 'breathe', and is therefore particularly appropriate for such porous building materials as lime renders, clay walling and stone, and on walls that are subject to damp (cellars and pantries). Limewash is best applied with a brush in thin coats, and a binder such as tallow, raw linseed oil or casein can be added to the mix to make it more durable. It dries lighter and brighter, making it virtually impossible to match one coloured limewash to another, so remember to mix sufficient quantities to complete the job. Various companies throughout the world now supply limewash (see p. 191).

graining

An age-old paint effect where inferior wood or other cheap materials such as tin are painted to resemble particular timbers. Hardwoods were generally left untreated and simply waxed; however, with the growing use of softwood at the end of the seventeenth century, timber was increasingly grained (stripped pine is very much a twentieth-century fashion). For the most part, graining simulates such hardwoods as oak, mahogany, walnut, rosewood and maple. At its finest, it is difficult to distinguish this technique from a real-wood surface.

The early-nineteenth century saw a revival of this art and much survives in country houses, especially in bedrooms or in the servants' quarters. Graining remained popular well into the twentieth century – many suburban front doors still resemble oak or another hardwood.

Materials for graining are still available and the art still practised. A top coat of scumble, an oil paint that comes in various colours – light, medium or dark oak and mahogany – is applied over a base coat of cream. Graining (or figuring) is achieved by combing or brushing the wet scumble, which is then varnished when dry.

glossary

Aga A large insulated stove with an enamel surface that can also provide central heating. Aga is a trade name and is synonymous with English country living.

Arched register plate grate A fire grate with an arched front and a semicircular plate at its rear to regulate the flow of air into and from the chimney.

Architrave The lowest section of an entablature. Its moulded profile is used to embellish door and window surrounds.

Barley-twist column The shaft of this type of column is turned in a continuous spiral. Used in sixteenth-century Italian architecture, it became popular again in the decoration of early-eighteenth-century stair balusters.

Bateau bed French in origin, the bed has curved ends to give the appearance of a boat.

Bergère chair A French design that uses woven cane to make the chair panels.

Bothy A small outhouse, usually heated by an open fire.

Butler's tray A large tray with vertical sides and a folding stand, used by household staff and butlers to bring food and drink from the kitchen into the 'polite' rooms of a house.

Capital The decorative cap of a column.

Casement window A window with frames that open outwards or inwards and which is hinged on one side.

Castello A small Italian castle.

Copper-plate engraving A type of engraving (print on paper) particularly popular in the eighteenth century, and created by applying sheets of paper to an inked copper plate engraved with a design or scene.

Commode A French term for a piece of furniture containing drawers or shelves. Also refers to a type of cabinet or chair with a hinged flap concealing a chamber pot.

Cornice The moulded top section of an entablature, used on top of doors and mantelpieces and to conceal the junction between wall and ceiling.

Craquelure A cracked effect on paint, varnish, such materials as leather or the surface of a piece of china.

Dado rail A moulded rail fixed to a wall at waist height. Also known as a chair rail, because it protected plaster walls from damage by the backs of chairs.

Distemper A lime-based wall and ceiling paint, commonly used before the advent of modern emulsion paints.

Dumbwaiter The name given to a pulley-driven lift that transports food from kitchen to dining room; or a stand with a central shaft and various circular levels for food and drink.

Empire A late version of neoclassicism popular during the empire of Napoleon Bonaparte (1804–15) and influential throughout Europe and North America.

Federal A style of decoration prevalent in the USA from the establishment of the Federal Government in 1789 and influenced for the most part by the English and French neoclassical movement.

Fielding The chamfering of the internal edges of panelling to give it a three-dimensional appearance.

Fillet A small, narrow and flat moulding often used on top of wallpaper or silk hangings to form a decorative border.

Firedog Either of a pair of iron stands to support logs in an open fire. These predate the fixed metal fire grate.

Flat oil paint An oil-based paint that has a totally sheen-free flat appearance.

Flock wallpaper Wallpaper that usually has embossed floral patterns. Traditionally created by applying glue onto the designed paper and then dusting the surface with coloured wool dust.

Frieze The horizontal and ornamental band between the architrave and cornice of a classical entablature. It is often decorated with such designs as humans and animals.

Gazebo A raised summer house or garden pavilion, sited to command a view and usually in a park or at the corner of a walled-garden.

Georgian A style of architecture and decoration associated with George I to IV (1714–1830) in England. For the most part classical in inspiration.

Gilding Gold leaf applied to timber, plaster or metal.

Glazing bar A timber or metal bar dividing a window into separate panes, while securing the glass in place.

Graining The painting, printing or staining of a surface in imitation of the grain of wood.

Hip bath A freestanding zinc, tin or iron bath in which the bather can sit but not lie. One side is higher than the others and forms a back rest.

Italianate Architecture inspired by and using certain decorative features of Italian classical design.

Jamb The vertical sides of a door or window frame.

Ladderback chair A type of English country chair, the back of which is constructed of horizontal slats between two uprights.

Lath One of several thin narrow strips of wood used to provide a supporting framework for such things as plaster.

Limewash Lime mixed with water and sometimes small amounts of such other materials as animal glue. The liquid is then used as a paint for stone, brick and plaster either internally or externally. Without the addition of pigments, the dried finish is called whitewash.

Lincrusta A type of decorative heavily embossed wallpaper, used on ceilings and walls below dado height.

Lintel A timber, stone or metal beam across the top of a window or door opening.

Majolica or maiolica A type of porous pottery glazed with bright metallic oxides. It was produced extensively in Renaissance Italy.

Ménagère A late-nineteenth-century trade name for bathroom fittings.

Mezzotint A method of engraving a copper plate by scraping and burnishing the roughened surface. Mezzotints are particularly noted for the subtlety of their tonal range from dark to light and, therefore, are used widely for portraiture.

Moulding A decorative shaped outline made of timber, plaster, stone or metal either cut out of or applied to such architectural elements as cornices or door architraves.

Mullion Vertical bars of timber, metal or masonry that divide the panes of a window.

Muntin and plank Timber panelling formed from vertical planks.

Newel The posts at the top and bottom of a staircase.

Palazzo An Italian palace.

Pantile An interlocking roof tile with an S-shaped cross section.

Parquet floor A timber floor made of small blocks of wood laid in a decorative pattern.

Plinth The rectangular slab or block that forms the base of a column or statue. It is also the flat block on either side of a doorframe where the architrave meets the skirting.

Press A cupboard, often large, used to store food or textiles.

Regency The style of furniture and decorative art prevalent in England during the regency of George IV (1811–20). A variety of neoclassicism.

Rococo A decorative style that evolved in Europe in the early eighteenth century and which is a lighter version of Baroque. Characterized by asymmetrical and playful ornament – curves, swags, scrolls, shells and foliage.

Roll-top bath A type of cast-iron bath, usually supported on four legs, with a characteristic rolled or curved rim. Popular in the late nineteenth and early twentieth centuries.

Sanitary wallpaper A type of wipeable wallpaper produced for bathrooms and WCs in the period between the two world wars. Frequently its design imitates tiles or brickwork.

Sash window A type of window found principally in the UK, the Netherlands and the USA. Two sashs placed one above the other can slide past each other to form an opening.

Scrap screen A folding screen onto which prints, scraps from magazines and bits of paper have been stuck.

Scumble The paint used to create the wood colour and effect of graining.

Slipper bath A moveable shallow bath made of zinc, tin or iron. Similar to a hip bath.

Square piano A type of rectangular piano that has the appearance of a table or sideboard.

Stucco A weather-resistant mixture of dehydrated lime, powdered marble and glue, used in decorative mouldings on buildings.

Ticking A tough cotton fabric used to cover mattresses and pillows. Intended to be hidden by linen or cotton covers, old ticking often has very attractive striped patterns.

Tooling Any decorative work done with a tool.

Trompe l'oeil Painted decoration on a flat surface intended to deceive the eye and to give the illusion of reality in three dimensions.

Turkey rug A knotted carpet with a deep pile and rich hues of red, blue and green. Of Turkish origin, these rugs were popular in the eighteenth and nineteenth centuries.

suppliers

conservation bodies

The Architectural Heritage Society of
Scotland
The Glasite Meeting House
33 Barony Street
Edinburgh EH3 6NX, UK
Tel: +44 (0)131 557 0019
Fax: +44 (0)131 557 0049

The Brooking Collection
Tel: +44 (0)1483 274 203
Charles Brooking offers a consultancy
service to help date, repair and reinstate
features. By appointment only.

Cadw – Welsh Historic Monuments
Cathays Park
Cardiff CF2 1UY, UK
Tel: +44 (0)2920 500 200
Fax: +44 (0)2920 826 375

Dúchas (The Heritage Service of the
Department of Arts, Heritage, Gaeltacht
and the Islands)
7 Ely Place
Dublin 2
Ireland
Tel: +353 1 647 3000
Fax: +353 1 662 0283

English Heritage
Fortress House
23 Savile Row
London W1S 2ET, UK
Tel: +44 (0)20 7973 3000
Fax: +44 (0)20 7973 3001

Fondation de Patrimoine (Heritage
Foundation)
Palais de Chaillot
1, place du Trocadéro
75116 Paris
France
Tel: +33 1 53 67 76 00

The Georgian Group
6 Fitzroy Square
London W1T 5DX, UK
Tel: +44 (0)20 7529 8920
Fax: +44 (0)20 7529 8939

Historic Houses Association
2 Chester Street
London SW1X 7BB, UK
Tel: +44 (0)20 7259 5688
Fax: +44 (0)20 7259 5590
www.hha.org.uk

The National Trust
36 Queen Anne's Gate
London SW1H 9AS, UK
Tel: +44 (0)20 7222 9251
Fax: +44 (0)20 7222 5097

National Trust for Historic Preservation
1785 Massachusetts Avenue, NW
Washington, DC 20036, USA
Tel: +1 202 588 6000
www.nationaltrust.org

Royal Commission on the Ancient and
Historical Monuments of England
National Monuments Record Centre
Kemble Drive
Swindon
Wiltshire SN2 2GZ, UK
Tel: +44 (0)1793 414600
Fax: +44 (0)1793 414606
www.rcahms.gov.uk

Society of Architectural Historians of
Great Britain
Andrew Martindale, Hon Secretary
Flat 4, 23 London Street
Edinburgh EH3 6LY, UK
www.sahgb.org.uk

Society of Architectural Historians, USA
1365 North Astor Street
Chicago
Illinois 60610, USA
Tel: +1 312 573 1365
Fax: +1 312 573 1141

Society for the Protection of
Ancient Buildings
37 Spital Square
London E1 6DY, UK
Tel: +44 (0)20 7377 1644
Fax: +44 (0)20 7247 5296
Practical information is available from the
society, including very good technical
pamphlets on repairing old buildings.

The Twentieth Century Society
70 Cowcross Street
London EC1M 6EJ, UK
Tel: +44 (0)20 7250 3857
Fax: +44 (0)20 7251 8985
www.c20society.demon.co.uk

Vieilles Maisons Françaises
91 rue Faubourg St. Honoré
75370 Paris
France
Tel: +33 1 42 66 00 12
Fax: +33 1 49 24 95 99

The Victorian Society
1 Priory Gardens
Bedford Park
London W4 1TT, UK
Tel: +44 (0)20 8994 1019
Fax: +44 (0)20 8747 5899
www.victorian-society.org.uk

architectural features and salvage

Architectural Heritage
Taddington Manor
Taddington, Nr. Cutsdean
Cheltenham
Gloucestershire GL54 5RY, UK
Tel: +44 (0)1386 584 414
Fax: +44 (0)1386 584 236
www.architectural-heritage.co.uk

Atelier Zimmermann
Chantepie
53320 Loiron
France
Tel: +33 2 43 02 12 81

Dorset Reclamation
Cow Drove
Bere Regis
Dorset BH20 7JZ, UK
Tel: +44 (0)1929 472200
Fax: +44 (0)1929 472292
www.dorsetreclamation.co.uk

Lassco
St Michael and All Angels Church
Mark Street
London EC2A 4ER, UK
Tel: +44 (0)20 7749 9944
www.lassco.co.uk

Les Matériaux Anciens Jean Chabaud
ZI Route de Gargas
84400 Apt-en-Provence
France
Tel: +33 4 90 74 07 61

Les Matériaux d'Autrefois
RN 113–34740 Vendargues
France
Tel: +33 4 67 70 15 72

Liz's Antique Hardware
453 S La Brea Avenue
Los Angeles
California 90036, USA
Tel: +1 323 939 4403

Pariscope
22 N. Third Street
Geneva
Illinois 60134, USA
Tel: +1 630 232 1600

Roméo
Showroom 2.10.12
Faubourg St Antoine
75012 Paris
France
Tel: +33 1 43 43 84 80

Salvage One
1840 W. Hubbard Street
Chicago
Illinois 06622, USA
Tel: +1 312 733 0098

Salvo Magazine
P.O. Box 28080
London SE27 0YZ, UK
Tel: +44 (0)20 8761 2316
www.salvoweb.com
www.wantsandoffers.com

Shabby Chic
1013 Montana Avenue
Santa Monica
California 90403, USA
Tel: +1 310 394 1975
(furniture)

Walcot Reclamation
108 Walcot Street
Bath BA1 5BG, UK
Tel: +44 (0)1225 444404
www.walcot.com

paint, limewash, graining, distemper

Craig & Rose
Unit 8
Halbeath Industrial Estate
Cross Gates Road
Dunfermline KY11 7EG, UK
Tel: +44 (0)1383 740 000
Fax: +44 (0)1383 740 010
(paint and lacquers)

Farrow and Ball
Uddens Estate
Wimborne
Dorset BH21 7NL, UK
Tel: +44 (0)1202 876 141
Fax: +44 (0)1202 873 793
www.farrow-ball.com
Showrooms also in Paris, New York
and Toronto
Tel (North America): +1 888 511 1121
(flat oil paint, distemper, limewash)

Foxell & James Ltd
57 Farringdon Road
London EC1 3JB, UK
Tel: +44 (0)20 7405 0152
Fax: +44 (0)20 7405 3631
(specialist paints and varnishes,
floor finishes)

The Real Paint & Varnish Company
Little Asby
Appleby-in-Westmorland
Cumbria CA16 6QE, UK

Tel: +44 (0)1539 623 662
www.realpaints.com
(paints, graining colours, limewash, distemper)

Rose of Jericho
Horchester Farm
Holywell, Nr. Evershot
Dorchester
Dorset DT2 0LL, UK
Tel: +44 (0)1935 83 676
Fax: +44 (0)1935 83 903
www.rose-of-jericho.demon.co.uk
(limewash)

gilding and specialist pigments

Cleton
41 rue Saint Sabin
75011 Paris
France
Tel: +33 1 47 00 10 41

A. P. Fitzpatrick
142 Cambridge Heath Road
Bethnal Green
London E1 5QJ, UK
Tel: +44 (0)20 7790 0884

Stuart R. Stevenson
68 Clerkenwell Road
London EC1M 5QA, UK
Tel: +44 (0)20 7253 1693
Fax: +44 (0)20 7490 0451

plaster decoration and casts

Atelier de moulages du Louvre
1 impasse du Pilier, 1 rue des Blés
93217 La Plaine Saint-Denis
France
Tel: +33 1 49 46 25 60
Fax: +33 1 49 46 95 34

British Museum Casts
British Museum shop
Great Russell Street
London WC1, UK
Tel: +44 (0)20 7323 8584
Fax: +44 (0)20 7580 8699

Peter Hone and Marianna Kennedy
3 Fournier Street
Spitalfields
London E1 6QE, UK
Tel: +44 (0)20 7375 2757
(decorative plaster medallions, casts, by
appointment only)

London Plastercraft
314 Wandsworth Bridge Road

London SW6 2UF, UK
Tel: +44 (0)20 7736 5146
Fax: +44 (0)20 7736 7190

painted and lacquered furniture

Bruno Charles
235 Avenue de-Lattre-de-Tassigny
34400 Lunel
France
Tel: +33 4 67 71 36 10
Fax: +33 4 67 71 58 40

Pedro da Costa Felgueiras and Marianna
Kennedy
3 Fournier Street
Spitalfields
London E1 6QE, UK
Tel: +44 (0)20 7375 2757
(by appointment only)

old pianos

Period Piano Company
Park Farm
Oast Hareplain Road
Biddenden
Kent TN27 8LJ, UK
Tel/fax: +44 (0)1580 291393
www.periodpiano.com

ceramics

Don Carpentier
104 Mud Pond Road
East Nassau
New York, USA
Tel: +1 518 766 2422

textiles

Baileys
The Engine Shed
Station Approach
Ross-On-Wye
Herefordshire HR9 7BW, UK
Tel: +44 (0)1989 563015
www.baileyshomeandgarden.com
(vintage and retro household goods)

Garry Conner
Tel: +44 (0)7899 731313
(antique linen)

Pierre Frey
47 rue des Petits Champs
75001 Paris
France
Tel: +33 1 44 77 36 00

Clarke Goldberg Textile Conservation
Tel: +44 (0)20 8447 1215

Robert Kime
121A Kensington Church Street
London W8 7LP, UK
Tel: +44 (0)20 7229 0886
Fax: +44 (0)20 7229 0766
(antique and other traditional textiles)

Ian Mankin
109 Regents Park Road
Primrose Hill
London NW1 8UR, UK
Tel: +44 (0)20 7722 0997
(ticking fabrics)

Danielle Mercier
Boisvieux
26210 Lapeyrouse
France
Tel: +33 4 75 31 82 58

Zoffany
Unit G9
Chelsea Harbour Design Centre
Chelsea Harbour
London SW10 0XE, UK
Tel: +44 (0)20 7349 0043
Fax: +44 (0)20 7351 9677
www.zoffany.com
(traditional wallpapers and fabrics)

ironmongery and fittings

Antique Stove Heaven
5414 S. Western Avenue
Los Angeles
California 90062, USA
Tel: +1 323 298 5582
(kitchen appliances)

Dickinson's Period House Shop
141 Corve Street
Ludlow

Shropshire SY8 2PG, UK
Tel: +44 (0)1584 877276

Farmer Brothers & JD Beardmore
Co Ltd
554 Kings Road
London SW6 2DZ, UK
Tel: +44 (0)20 7371 5881
Fax: +44 (0)20 7736 3671
(traditional ironmongery)

Grand Brass Lamp Parts
26 Meadow Street
Brooklyn
New York 11206, USA
Tel: +1 212 226 2567
(light fittings)

Heartland Appliances Inc.
1050 Fountain Street North
Cambridge, Ontario
Canada N3H 4R7
Tel: +1 800 361 1517
(kitchen appliances)

Rejuvenation Hardware
1100 S.E. Grand Avenue
Portland
Oregon 97214, USA
Tel: +1 503 238 1900

The Shutter Shop
Unit 3, Taplins Court
Church Lane
Hartley Wintney
Hampshire RG27 8XU, UK
Tel: +44 (0)1252 844575
Fax: +44 (0)1252 844718
www.shuttershop.co.uk
(louvre shutters)

Urban Archaeology
239 East 58th Street
New York
New York 10022, USA

Tel: +1 212 371 4646
(bathroom fixtures)

wall and floor surfaces

Crucial Trading
79 Westbourne Park Road
London W2 5QH, UK
Tel: +44 (0)20 7221 9000

Waveney Rush Industry
The Old Maltings
Caldecott Road, Oulton Broad
Lowestoft
Suffolk NR32 3PH, UK
Tel: +44 (0)1502 538 777
Fax: +44 (0)1502 538 477
E-mail: crafts@waveneyrush.co.uk
www.waveneyrush.co.uk

wallpaper

Adelphi
P.O. Box 494
The Plains
Virginia 20198-0494, USA
Tel: +1 540 253 5367
Fax: +1 540 253 5388
www.adelphipaperhangings.com
(reprints of historical French, English and
American wallpapers using traditional
block printing)

Bradbury & Bradbury
P.O. Box 155
Benicia
California 94510, USA
Tel: +1 707 746 1900
Fax: +1 707 745 9417
www.bradbury.com
(reprints of Victorian, Arts & Crafts
and neoclassical wallpapers)

Colefax and Fowler
39 Brook Street
London W1K 4JE, UK
Tel: +44 (0)20 7493 2231
Fax: +44 (0)20 7355 4037
Worldwide stockists:
+44 (0)20 8874 6484

de Gournay
112 Old Church Street
London SW3 6EP, UK
Tel: +44 (0)20 7823 7316
Fax: +44 (0)20 7823 7475
(reproductions of early-nineteenth-
century scenic French wallpapers)

Hamilton Weston
18 St Mary's Grove
Richmond

Surrey TW9 1UY, UK
Tel: +44 (0)20 8940 4850
(reprints of historical French, English and
American wallpapers using traditional
block printing)

The Irish Georgian Group
74 Merrion Square
Dublin
Ireland
Tel: +353 1 676 7053
Fax: +353 1 662 0290
(print-room borders)

Sanderson
233 Kings Road
London SW3 5EJ, UK
Tel: +44 (0)1895 83 0044
www.sanderson-uk.com
(collections of original wallpapers
designed by William Morris and available
as surface printed designs)

John Sutcliffe
12 Huntingdon Road
Cambridge CB3 0HH, UK
Tel/fax: +44 (0)1223 315 858
(print-room borders)

Wallpaper History Society
Gill Saunders
c/o The Victoria and Albert Museum
Exhibition Road
London SW7 2RL, UK
Tel: +44 (0)20 7942 2560

Zuber
28 Rue Zuber
68170 Rixheim
France
Tel: +33 3 89 44 13 88
New York: +1 212 486 9226
London: +44 (0)20 7824 8265
Los Angeles: +1 310 652 5174
(hand-printed wallpaper and fabrics)

fireplaces

Chesneys
194–202 Battersea Park Road
London SW11 4ND, UK
Tel: +44 (0)20 7627 1410
www.chesneys.co.uk

Chesneys New York
D&D Building
Suite 244, 2nd Floor
979 Third Avenue
New York, NY 10022, USA
Tel: +1 646 840 0609

featured houses

Calke Abbey, Ticknall, Derbyshire, UK
(a National Trust property)

Sea-captain's house, Whitechapel,
East London, UK

Silkweaver's house, Spitalfields, London, UK

Manor house, near Shrewsbury, Shropshire, UK

Timber-framed farmhouse, North
Shropshire, UK

Medieval French château, near Clermont-
Ferrand, Auvergne, France

French château, near Vichy, France

Apartment, Turin, Italy

Palazzo, near Turin, Italy

Palazzo, Turin, Italy

Castello, near Turin, Italy

Tenement building, East Berlin, Germany

House, Potsdam, Germany

Castletown, Celbridge, near Dublin, Ireland
(with kind permission of Dúchas, The
Heritage Service of the Department of Arts,
Heritage, Gaeltacht and the Islands)

Townhouse, Dublin, Ireland

Country house, near Dublin, Ireland

Schoolhouse, near Dublin, Ireland

Killadoon, Celbridge, near Dublin, Ireland

Aitken-Rhett House, Charleston, South
Carolina, USA (a property of the Historic
Charleston Foundation)

Drayton Hall, near Charleston, South
Carolina, USA (a property of the National
Trust for Historic Preservation, USA)

Apartment, East Village, New York, USA